101

3-4 Defense Drills

James Pavao

COACHES
CHOICE™

ISBN: 978-1-60679-252-0
Library of Congress Control Number: 2012955923
Cover design: Cheery Sugabo
Book layout: Bean Creek Studio
Front cover photo: Getty Images
Chapter page graphic: Hemera/Thinkstock

Coaches Choice
P.O. Box 1828
Monterey, CA 93942
www.coacheschoice.com

Dedication

To my mom and dad, thank you for being a fantastic example of what it takes to be a great parent. To my brothers, Gary and Dennis, it was wonderful growing up with you guys. To my children, Nicholas, Lauren, Neil, and Andrew, God blessed me with four incredible children. To my wife, Sally, I will love you forever—you are my best friend in the world.

Acknowledgments

I would like to thank God for placing me in the great profession of coaching. I would also like to thank Barry Mynter for giving me my first job at Norwich University and Phil Wilks for mentoring me for 13 years while at Maryville College. You have both made a huge difference in my life.

Contents

1

Pre-Practice Drills

Drill #1: Throw and Catch

Objective: To develop the linebackers and defensive backs catching ability

Equipment Needed: Six balls

Description: In this drill, the players are in two lines, 10 yards apart. The players will throw the ball back and forth to each other. During this time, you can check attendance and review fronts and coverage checks.

Coaching Points:
- The players should catch the ball with two hands.
- The players should tuck the ball away after catching it.

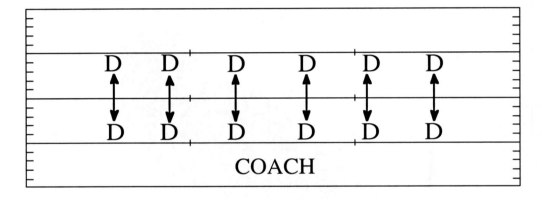

Drill #2: Front

Objective: To review fronts and stunts with the defensive lineman and linebackers

Equipment Needed: Five tires, one ball

Description: Place the five tires on a yard line aligned as an offensive line. The front seven align in front of the tires, facing the coach. The coach calls a front or stunt. The linebackers go through all the pre-snap calls and adjustments. On the coach's command "Stance," all seven players assume proper stance and alignment. On ball movement, all seven players execute their assignment. Go through all fronts and stunts. Repeat the drill with the next group.

Coaching Points:
- The players should be in a good stance.
- The players should move full speed for three steps.
- The players should move low and finish in a low stance.

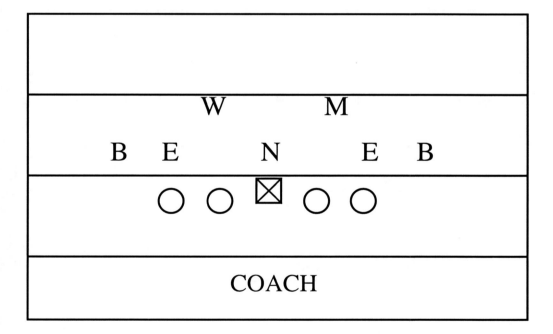

Drill #3: Formation Recognition

Objective: To teach and review formations and motion adjustments with the linebackers and defensive backs

Equipment Needed: Five cones

Description: Place six players in an offensive formation. The defensive players align to the formation based on the coverage called. On the coach's command "stance," all players assume their proper stance and alignment. On the go command, all players execute their read steps. Change formations, add motion and tight end trades. Repeat for five to six reps. Rotate players.

Coaching Points:
- The players should be in a good stance.
- The players should make all pre-snap call and checks.

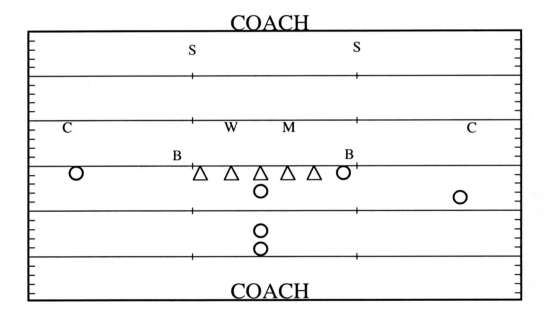

Drill #4: Spar

Objective: To develop the defensive linemen's and outside linebackers' pass rush skills

Equipment Needed: None

Description: The players align across from a partner two yards apart. On the go command, the offensive player will get in a stance with his knees bent and his arms up. The defensive player will begin to execute a series of club-and-rip, club-and-swim, spin, fake, and go rush moves. The offensive player will turn around and face the defensive player after the move is completed.

Coaching Points:
- The defensive players should focus on technique rather than speed in this drill.
- The players will have very limited contact in this drill.
- Each player will have 10 seconds to work rush moves.
- The defender should execute the rush move to the right and left of the blocker.

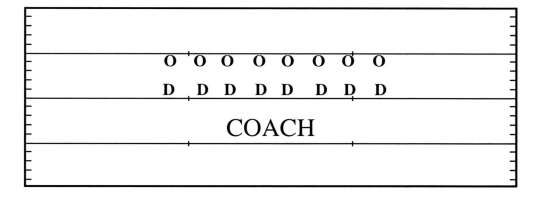

Drill #5: Hot Potato

Objective: To develop the defensive backs' and linebackers' reaction and concentration on the football

Equipment Needed: One ball

Description: The defender stands 15 yards away from the coach with his back turned. The coach makes a ball call, and the defender quickly turns around with his hands up ready to catch the ball. The coach will throw the ball on the ball call. After the defender catches the ball, he should make an "Oskie" call, tuck the ball away, and run the ball back to the coach. Repeat the drill with the next player in line.

Coaching Points:
- The player should look the ball into his hands.
- The player should always catch the ball with two hands.
- The player should tuck the ball away after he catches the ball.
- Shorten the distance to 10 yards, when the players get good at 15 yards.

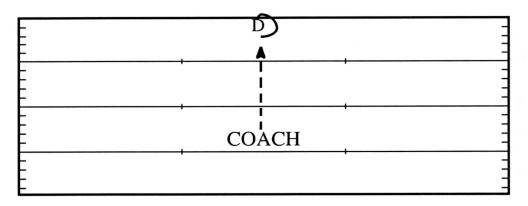

Drill #6: High Ball

Objective: To teach the defensive backs how to catch the football at the ball's high point

Equipment Needed: Three balls

Description: The defensive backs get in a single line on the side, and the coach is standing at the hash. On the go command, the defensive back runs from the sideline toward the numbers. When the defensive back gets near the numbers, the coach will throw a high ball near the numbers. The defensive back should come to balance, and then time a jump to catch the ball at its high point. When he catches the ball, he should yell "Oskie," tuck the ball away, and run it back to the coach.

Coaching Points:
- The players should go up for the ball with two hands.
- The players should catch the ball at its high point.
- The players should yell "Oskie" after they catch the ball.
- The players should tuck the ball away after they catch the ball.

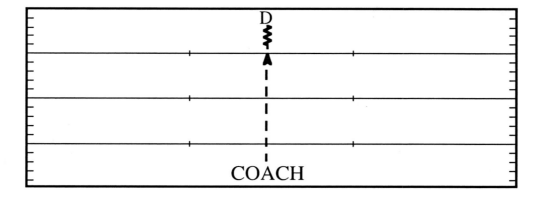

2

Tackling Drills

Drill #7: Form Tackle (Head-Up)

Objective: To teach and develop the correct tackling form

Equipment Needed: None

Description: The players will align in two lines. The ballcarrier will stand on the yard line. The tackler should be one step from the ballcarrier. On the command "stance," the players assume a good two-point stance. On the go command, the tackler takes a six-inch jab step and clubs his arms up from the hip. The player should wrap his arms in the back and grab high cloth. The player should step with the right foot for two repetitions, and then step with the left foot for two repetitions. When the first group completes their repetitions, rotate the drill. Repeat the drill from three steps apart, then five steps apart.

Coaching Points:
- The tackler should be in a good stance.
- The tackler should take a short jab step.
- The tackler should club arm his arm up and grab cloth.
- The tackler should make contact with his upper chest to the ballcarrier's low chest.
- The tackler should keep his eyes up.
- The tackler should hit on the rise and keep his feet chopping.

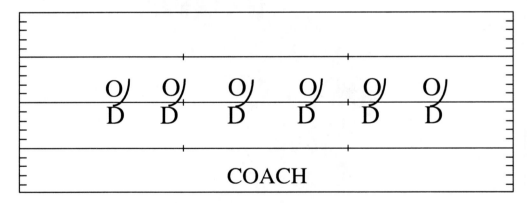

Drill #8: Form Tackle (Angle Tackle)

Objective: To teach the proper angle tackling technique

Equipment Needed: None

Description: The players should form two lines, the ballcarrier will stand on the yard line, and the tackler will offset one step to the right of the ballcarrier. On the command "stance," the players assume a good two-point stance. On the go command, the tackler takes a six-inch jab step with his left foot. The tackler should place his head across the ballcarrier's body, making contact with his right shoulder. On contact, the tackler should club his arms and grab cloth. The tackle will get two repetitions with the right shoulder, and then two repetitions with the left shoulder. Rotate the groups, and then repeat the drill from three steps apart, and then five steps apart.

Coaching Points:
- The tackler should assume a good stance.
- The tackler should take a six-inch jab step.
- The tackler's head should be across the body of the ballcarrier.
- The tackler should club arms up and grab cloth.
- The tackler should extend his hips and keep his feet chopping.

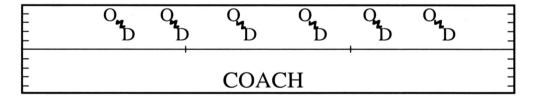

Drill #9: Shimmy Tackle

Objective: To develop the defensive players' ability to break down in the open field and make a tackle

Equipment Needed: None

Description: Four lines of players, the ballcarrier will line up on the sideline, and the tackler will line up on the numbers. On the command "stance," the tacklers will assume a proper two-point stance. On the whistle, the tackler will close the gap between him and the ballcarrier. When the tackler is three yards from the ballcarrier, he will drop his hips, widen, and buzz his feet, continuing to close the gap between him and the ballcarrier. When the tackler gets to the ballcarrier, he should club his arms up from the hips, grab high cloth, and roll his hips and continue to shimmy. Rotate the players after each repetition.

Coaching Points:
- The tackler should be in a good stance.
- The tackler should close the gap quickly, and then drop his hips and buzz his feet.
- The tackler should keep his eyes on the ballcarrier's belt.
- The tackler should use short, quick shimmy steps through the tackle and continue feet chopping until the whistle blows.

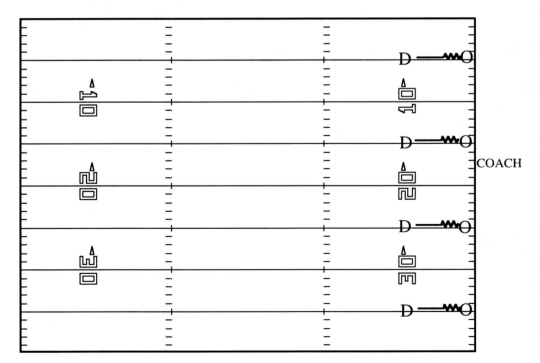

Drill #10: Open Field Tackle

Objective: To teach and develop the defensive players' open field tackling ability

Equipment Needed: None

Description: Align the ballcarriers on the sideline in three separate lines. Align the tacklers on the hash in three lines across from the ballcarriers. On the whistle, both players begin running toward each other. The tackler should close the gap as quickly as possible. When the tackler gets three to five yards away from the ballcarrier, he will drop his hips, widen his feet, and shimmy his feet. The ballcarrier can make one move in the five-yard space. The tackler should slide to the left or right, put his head across, and club his arms to make the tackle.

Coaching Points:
- The tackler should close the gap quickly.
- The tackler should break down and shimmy his feet, and keep his eyes on the ballcarrier's belt.
- The tackler should slide—not lunge—to the tackle.
- The tackler should club his arms up, and grab cloth.

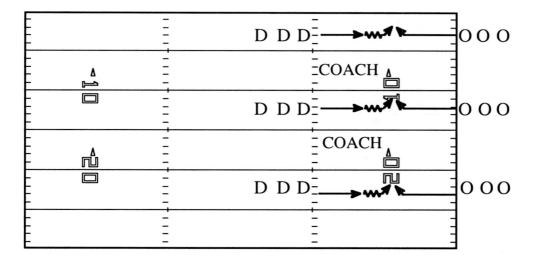

Drill #11: Sweep Tackle

Objective: To teach and develop defensive players to take the proper angle of pursuit, and to tackle a ballcarrier on a wide play

Equipment Needed: Three cones

Description: Place two cones 10 yards apart on the hash. Place the third cone six yards from the sideline. The players should split into two groups on the hash. When the whistle blows, the ballcarrier should begin to run toward the sideline and start to turn it up as he approaches the cone. The tackler will shuffle-step, and then angle-run toward the ballcarrier. When the tackler closes the gap, he should execute an angle tackle.

Coaching Points:
- The tackle should be in a good two-point stance.
- The tackler should keep inside leverage on the ballcarrier.
- The tackler should place his head across and club his arms upward.
- The tackler should keep his head up, keep his feet running, and grab cloth.

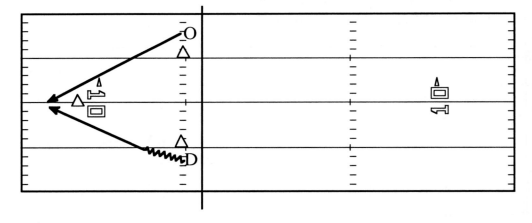

Drill #12: Goal Line Tackle

Objective: To develop the defensive players' ability to tackle in a short yardage and goal line situation

Equipment Needed: Three cones, one ball

Description: Place two cones on the goal line four yards apart. Place the third cone on the four-yard line. The ballcarrier should align in front of the cone on the four-yard line. The tackler should align between the two cones on the goal line. On the whistle, the ballcarrier will try to score between the two cones and crossing the goal line. The tackler should attack the ballcarrier with low pad level and execute a strong head-up tackle. The drill ends either when the ballcarrier scores or when he is tackled.

Coaching Points:
- The tackler should be in a good stance.
- The tackler should attack the ballcarrier and club his arms up violently.
- The tackler should keep his legs driving until the ballcarrier goes to the ground.

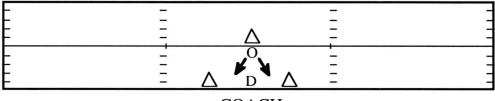

COACH

Drill #13: Lever and Tackle

Objective: To teach and develop the players' ability to get off a block and make a tackle

Equipment Needed: Two cones

Description: Place the two cones five yards apart. Break the players up into three groups: a tackler's line, a blocker's line, and a ballcarrier's line. The tackler fits into the blocker, placing his mask and hands into the blocker's chest. On the whistle, the defender executes a push-pull move, disengages from the blocker, and executes an angle tackle on the ballcarrier.

Coaching Points:
- The tackler should fit into the blocker in a low position.
- The tackler should push the blocker off him, and then with a quick pull throw the blocker to one side.
- The tackler should explode off the blocker to the ballcarrier.
- The tackler should club his arms up and run his feet on contact with the ballcarrier.

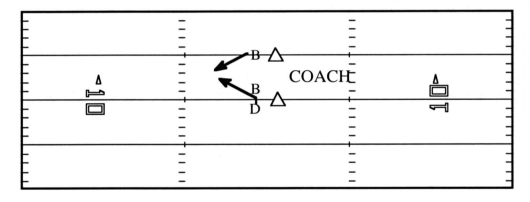

3

Defensive Line Drills

Drill #14: Stance and Start

Objective: To develop and teach the defensive linemen the proper stance and start technique

Equipment Needed: One ball

Description: Align the defensive linemen on a yard line five yards apart. Teach the stance in three steps. Step one: feet shoulder-width apart, toes pointed straight ahead. Step two: bend at the ankles, knees, and waist, and place their elbows on their knees. Step three: the players should lean forward and place the fingertips of both hands on the ground slightly in front of their mask. The hips should be slightly above their shoulders, neck bowed, eyes on the target. On ball movement, the players should take a six-inch power step and shoot their hands forward with thumbs up.

Coaching Points:
- The player's weight should be a 50:50 ratio of hands to feet.
- Teach a 45-degree-angle power step with the right and left feet.
- Teach a three-power-step move and then footfire, where the player runs his feet till the whistle blows.

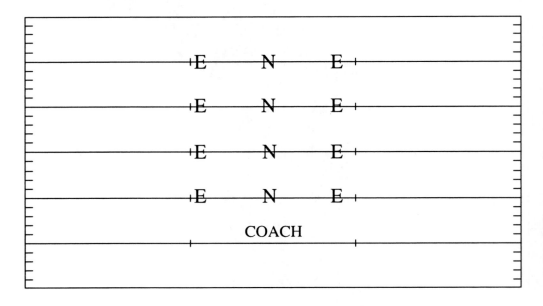

Drill #15: Hand Shiver—Six-Point Progression

Objective: To develop the defensive linemen's ability to deliver a blow on a blocker

Equipment Needed: Five-man sled (or three shields), one ball

Description: The players should face the sled in a six-point stance (toes, knees, and hands) on the ground, coiled back six inches from the pad. On ball movement, the players should shoot their hands at the pad with their thumbs pointed up. The heels of their hands and mask should hit the pad, and they should press their arm's out and roll their hips. Repeat for three repetitions, and switch groups. Then move to a four-point-stance explosion technique.

Coaching Points:
- The players should strike the pad with the heels of their hands and their thumbs pointing upward.
- The players should grab the pad and press.
- When the players perform the four-point explosion, their feet should keep chopping until the whistle blows.

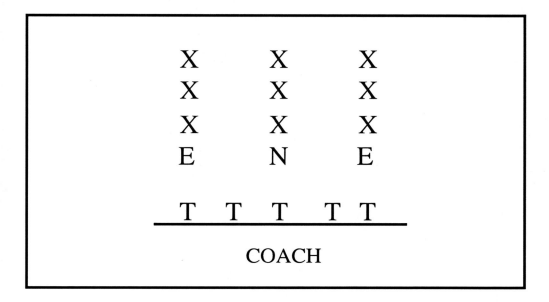

Drill #16: Lever and Pull

Objective: To develop the defensive linemen's ability to disengage from a blocker

Equipment Needed: None

Description: Three groups of defensive linemen align five yards apart. On the coach's command "fit," the defender places his mask and hands in the blocker's chest, getting in a low fit position. On the whistle, the defender thrusts his hips, runs his feet, and locks his arms out. When the defender feels the blocker lean forward, he should pull and throw the blocker to the right side and disengage with a quick arm over to the left. Execute three repetitions, and then repeat the drill to the right.

Coaching Points:
- Have the defender knock the blocker back with an aggressive hip thrust and push press.
- When the blocker leans forward, the defender should pull the blocker to the side.
- The defender must clear the block and accelerate off the block.

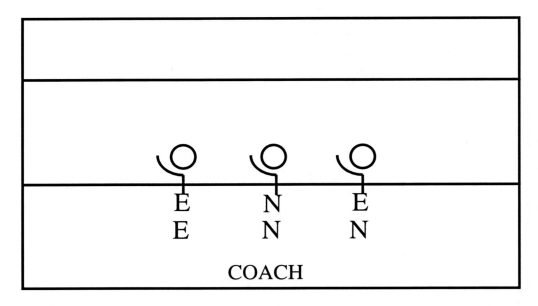

Drill #17: Lever and Rip

Objective: To develop the defensive linemen's ability to disengage from a blocker

Equipment Needed: None

Description: Three groups of defensive linemen align five yards apart. On the coach's command "fit," the defender places his mask and hands in the blocker's chest, getting in a low fit position. On the whistle, the defender thrusts his hips, runs his feet, and locks his arms out. When the defender feels the blocker lean backward, he should dip his right shoulder and rip his arm under the armpit of the blocker to the left. Execute three repetitions, and then repeat the drill to the right.

Coaching Points:
- Have the defender knock the blocker back with an aggressive hip thrust and push press.
- When the blocker leans backward, the defender should dip and rip to the side.
- The defender must clear the block and accelerate off the block.

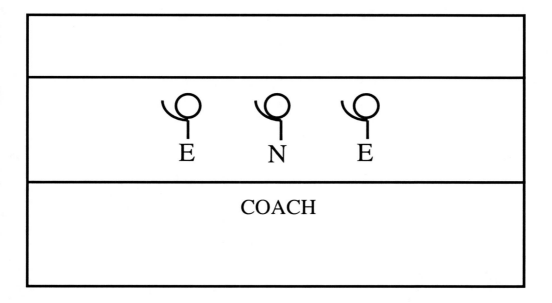

Drill #18: Board

Objective: To develop the defensive linemen's ability to defeat the base block and to evaluate the players physical toughness

Equipment Needed: Three 1" x 12" x 6' wood planks

Description: Align a defender and a blocker at opposite ends of the wood planks. On the whistle, both players attack each other. The drill continues until one of the players is knocked off the board.

Coaching Points:
- The players should fire out low.
- The players should hand shiver and lock out the blocker.
- The players should keep their feet chopping.

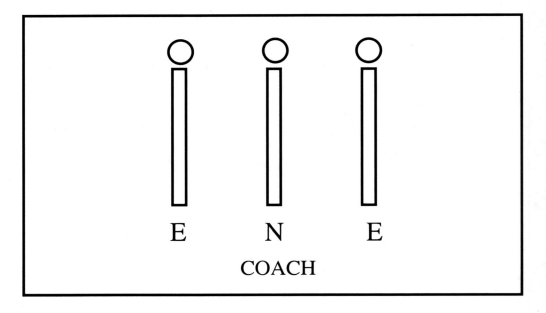

Drill #19: Slant Technique

Objective: To teach and develop the defensive linemen's ability to slant and angle

Equipment Needed: Three tires, one ball

Description: The defensive linemen align by position on one of three tires set five yards apart, on a yard line. The first player in each line assumes a four-point stance. On the ball movement, each player will execute a proper slant technique to the right. Repeat the drill to the left. Slanting to the right, the player should take a 45-degree angle step with his right foot. The second step is an upfield step while dipping the shoulder and ripping the arm through. On the third step, the player should square up in the hole.

Coaching Points:
- The player should grab grass on the rip.
- Have the player redirect right or left.

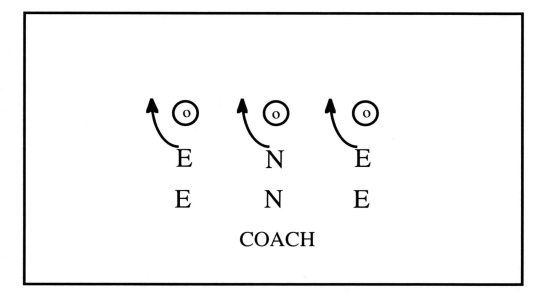

Drill #20: Pinch Technique

Objective: To teach and develop the defensive end's pinch technique

Equipment Needed: Three tires, one ball

Description: The defensive ends align on one of three tires set five yards apart, on a yard line. The first player in each line assumes a four-point stance. On the ball movement, each player will execute a proper pinch technique to the right. Repeat the drill to the left. Pinching to the right, the player should take a 45-degree angle step with his right foot. The second step should continue upfield, while dipping the shoulder and ripping the arm through. The ends aiming point is the hip of the guard.

Coaching Points:
- The player should grab grass on the rip.
- Have the player redirect right or left.

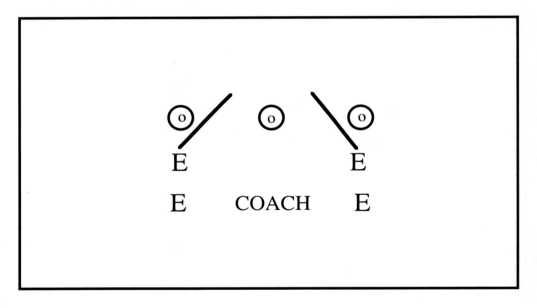

Drill #21: 1-on-1 Reach Block

Objective: To develop the defensive linemen's ability to defeat the reach block

Equipment Needed: None

Description: The defensive linemen align by position in three groups five yards apart. The coach hand signals to the blocker which direction to simulate the reach block. On the whistle, the three blockers simulate the block. On the blocker's movement, the defensive linemen should power-step with the playside foot, attack the blocker, and hand shiver him. The linemen should keep fighting pressure, and press and lock out the blocker. They should continue to fight down the line and disengage with a push-pull move. Rotate the groups, and repeat the drill.

Coaching Points:
- The defenders should power-step and hand shiver the blocker.
- The defender should keep his feet driving on contact.
- The defender should attack the blocker.

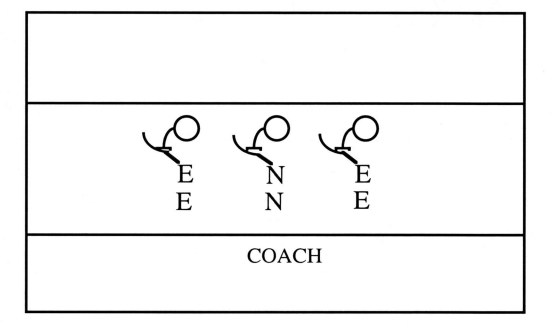

Drill #22: 2-on-1 Scoop

Objective: To develop the defensive linemen's ability to defeat the scoop block

Equipment Needed: None

Description: The defensive linemen align by position in three groups five yards apart. The coach hand signals to the blocker which direction to simulate the reach block. On the whistle, the blockers simulate the block. On the blocker's movement, the defensive linemen should power-step with the playside foot, attack the playside blocker, and hand shiver him. The linemen should keep fighting pressure, press, lock out and grab the blocker. They should continue to fight down the line of scrimmage, as this will not allow the backside blocker to get his head across the lineman's body. Rotate the groups, and repeat the drill.

Coaching Points:
- The defenders should power-step and hand shiver the playside blocker.
- The defender should keep his feet moving on contact.
- The defender should grab the playside blocker.
- The defender should run down the line of scrimmage.

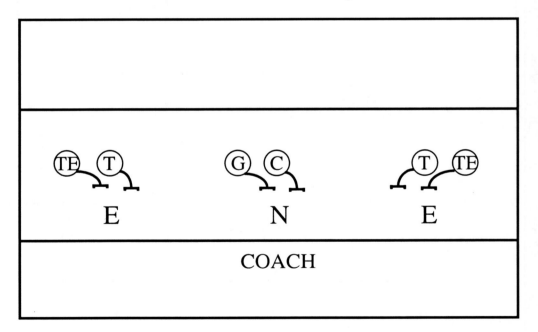

Drill #23: 2-on-1 Double-Team

Objective: To develop the defensive linemen's ability to defeat the double-team block

Equipment Needed: None

Description: The defensive linemen align by position in three groups five yards apart. The coach hand signals to the blocker which direction to simulate the double-team block. On the whistle, the blockers simulate the block. On the blocker's movement, the defensive linemen should power-step with the playside foot, attack the blocker, and hand shiver him. The linemen should keep fighting pressure, press, and lock out the blocker. When the defender feels outside pressure, he should turn his hips into him. If the defender gets continuous outside pressure, he should drop his outside knee and shoulder splitting the two blockers. Rotate the groups, and repeat the drill.

Coaching Points:
- The defenders should power-step and hand shiver the playside blocker.
- The defender should keep his feet moving on contact.
- The defender should play with low pads.
- The defender should make a pile if he feels he is losing ground.

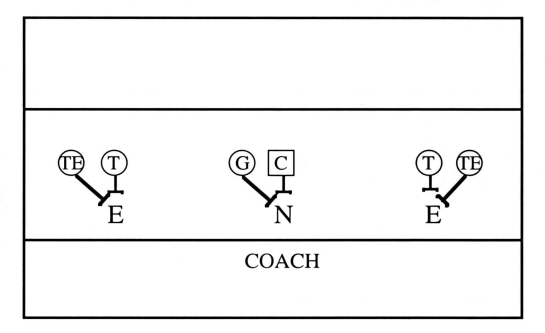

Drill #24: 2-on-1 Down Block

Objective: To develop the defensive linemen's ability to defeat the down block

Equipment Needed: None

Description: The defensive linemen align by position in three groups five yards apart. The coach hand signals to the blocker which direction to simulate the down block. On the whistle, the blockers simulate the block. On the blocker's movement, the defensive linemen should power-step with the playside foot, attack the blocker, and hand shiver him. The linemen should keep fighting pressure down the line of scrimmage, thinking trap. When the defender feels outside pressure, he should drive upfield and disrupt any pulling lineman. Rotate the groups, and repeat the drill.

Coaching Points:
- The defenders should power-step and hand shiver the playside blocker.
- The defender should keep his feet moving on contact.
- The defender should play with low pads.
- The defender should drive upfield when he feels the outside down block.

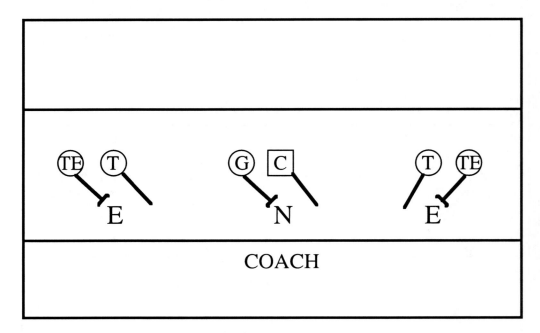

Drill #25: 3-on-1 Run Reads

Objective: To develop the defensive linemen's ability to defeat the double-team, down, reach (zone), and scoop blocks

Equipment Needed: None

Description: Three groups of three blocks five yards apart. The defensive linemen align on the middle blocker. The coach directs the blockers which blocking scheme to simulate. The three blockers execute the blocking scheme on the snap count. The defensive linemen should attack the blockers and defeat the block buy fighting through pressure.

Coaching Points:
- The coach should teach all the players how to perform the different blocks.
- The players should attack the blocks with low pads.
- The players should keep pads square to the line of scrimmage.
- The defender should fight through pressure.

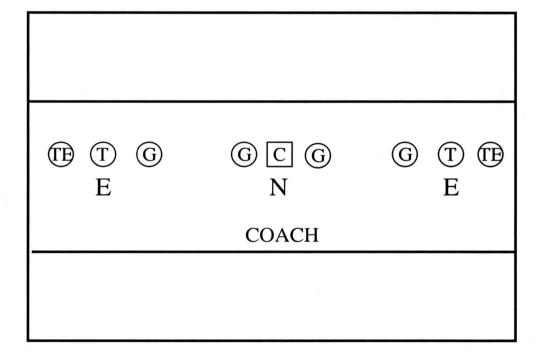

Drill #26: Trap the Trapper

Objective: To teach and develop the defensive linemen's ability and technique to play the trap play

Equipment Needed: None

Description: Align five offensive linemen and a fullback in an offensive formation. The coach should point out the trap scheme to the left or right, and give a snap count. On the snap, the blockers should execute the trap scheme. On the snap, the ends should power-step with their inside foot, hand shiver and squeeze the tackle down the line of scrimmage, and look inside for the next player to show. If it is the trapping guard, the end should attack the blocker with his outside shoulder and forearm (wrong arm technique) and punch through the block and wheel upfield to the ballcarrier. The nose should power-step and attack the center; when he feels the guard double-teaming him, he should turn his hip into the block. Then, he should attempt to split the block by dropping his playside knee and shoulder to the guard.

Coaching Points:
- The end should stay on the line of scrimmage and squeeze to the center, looking for the next man to hit.
- The nose should split the double-team, but if he can't, he should drop to the ground and make a pile. He can't get driven back.

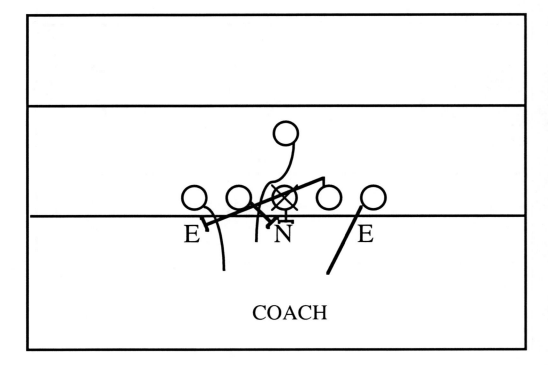

Drill #27: Takeoff

Objective: To improve the defensive linemen's pass rush takeoff

Equipment Needed: None

Description: Align three offensive players on a yard line five yards apart, with a defender aligned over them. The coach should hand signal the snap count to the offensive players. On the snap, the three offensive players should pass set as deep and as quickly as they can. The three defenders should attack and close the gap between them and the offensive player. The drill ends when the defender tags the offensive player.

Coaching Points:
- The defender should close on the blocker's first movement.
- The defender should have good body lean forward, like a sprinter.
- The defender should close the gap and tag the blocker as quickly as possible.

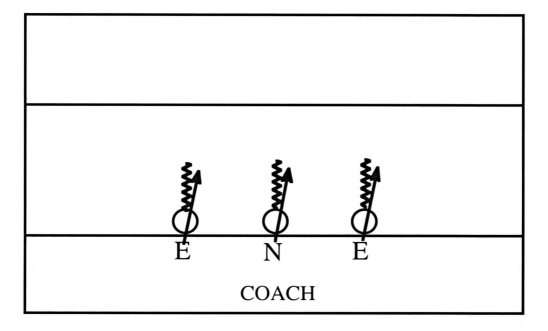

Drill #28: Bull Rush

Objective: To teach and develop the defensive linemen's ability to rush the passer with the bull rush

Equipment Needed: One stand-up dummy, two tires

Description: Three offensive linemen align on a yard line—one as the center, and two as tackles. Place the two tires as guards for proper spacing, and the dummy seven yards behind the center as the quarterback. The left end should fit in to the tackle with three points of contact. On the whistle, the defender will drive his feet, lock his arms out, and drive the blocker back to the dummy. The nose is second, and the right end is third. Repeat the drill sequence.

Coaching Points:
- The defender should fit in with low pad level.
- The defender should have his hands and mask in the blocker's chest.
- The defender should grab the breast plate of the blocker's shoulder pads.
- The defender should keep his feet driving until he reaches the dummy.

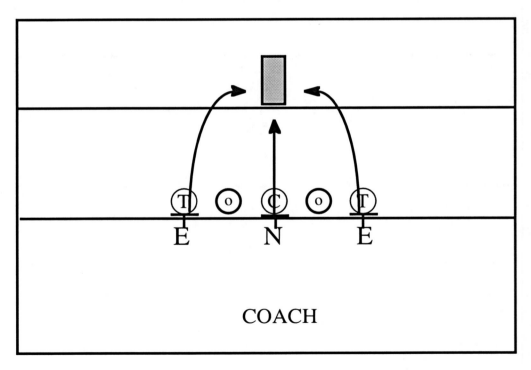

Drill #29: Bull and Rip Rush

Objective: To teach and develop the defensive linemen's ability to rush the passer with the bull and rip rush move

Equipment Needed: One stand-up dummy, two tires

Description: Three offensive linemen align on a yard line—one as the center, and two as tackles. Place the two tires as guards for proper spacing, and the dummy seven yards behind the center as the quarterback. The left end should fit in to the tackle with three points of contact. On the whistle, the defender will drive his feet, lock his arms out, and drive the blocker back. As the defender closes on the dummy, he should pull with the outside arm, rip under the blocker's armpit, and accelerate to the dummy. The nose is second, and the right end is third. Repeat the drill sequence.

Coaching Points:
- The defender should fit in with low pad level.
- The defender should have his hands and mask in the blocker's chest.
- The defender should grab the breast plate of the blocker's shoulder pads.
- The defender should use the rip move if he can get the blocker's shoulders turned.
- The defender should keep his feet driving until he reaches the dummy.

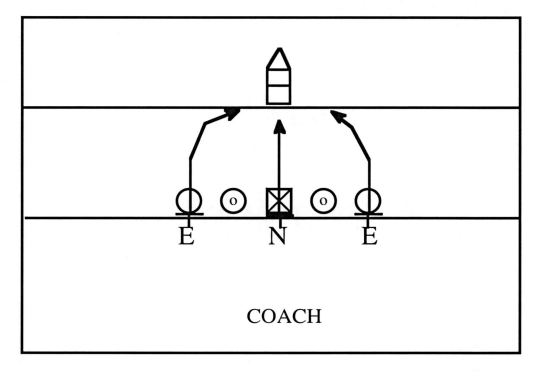

Drill #30: Bull and Pull Rush

Objective: To teach and develop the defensive linemen's ability to rush the passer with the bull and pull rush move

Equipment Needed: One stand-up dummy, two tires

Description: Three offensive linemen align on a yard line—one as the center, and two as tackles. Place the two tires as guards for proper spacing, and the dummy seven yards behind the center as the quarterback. The left end should fit in to the tackle with three points of contact. On the whistle, the defender will drive his feet, lock his arms out, and drive the blocker back. As the defender closes on the dummy, he pulls the blocker across his body with a quick pulling motion, and accelerates to the dummy. The nose is second, and the right end is third. Repeat the drill sequence.

Coaching Points:
- The defender should fit in with low pad level.
- The defender should have his hands and mask in the blocker's chest.
- The defender should grab the breast plate of the blocker's shoulder pads.
- The defender should keep his feet driving until he reaches the dummy.
- The defender should pull and throw the blocker to the side when he feels the blocker dropping his hips and leaning forward.

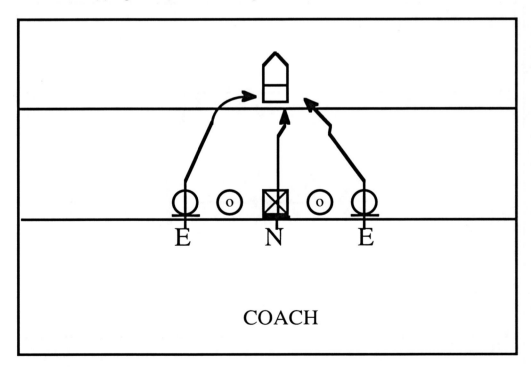

Drill #31: Bull and Spin Counter

Objective: To teach and develop the defensive linemen's ability to rush the passer with the bull and spin as a counter rush move when they are being run past the quarterback

Equipment Needed: One stand-up dummy, two tires

Description: Three offensive linemen align on a yard line—one as the center, and two as tackles. Place the two tires as guards for proper spacing, and the dummy seven yards behind the center as the quarterback. The left end should fit in to the tackle with three points of contact. On the whistle, the defender will drive his feet, lock his arms out, and drive the blocker back. As the defender closes on the dummy, but is passing it, he should drop his hips, lean into the blocker, and whip his body around to execute a spin move and accelerate to the dummy. The nose is second, and the right end is third. Repeat the drill sequence.

Coaching Points:
- The defender should fit in with low pad level.
- The defender should have his hands and mask in the blocker's chest.
- The defender should grab the breast plate of the blocker's shoulder pads.
- The defender should keep his feet driving and spin as a counter move.
- The defender should spin tight to the blocker and seal the blocker by whipping his arm and leg around.

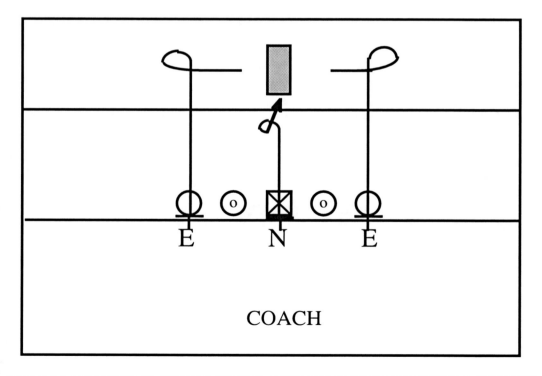

4

Inside Linebacker Drills

Drill #32: Stance and Alignment

Objective: To develop the linebacker's stance and alignment

Equipment Needed: Five tires

Description: Align the five tires on a yard line, one yard apart. The linebackers should align in two lines on the outside shoulder of the guard (30 technique). On the command "stance," all the linebackers should get into their stance. The players should hold their stance until given the "break" command. Repeat the drill for five or six repetitions.

Coaching Points:
- The linebacker should have his feet slightly wider than shoulder-with apart, and his toes should be pointed forward.
- The defender's ankles and knees should be flexed.
- The player should have his weight forward on the balls of his feet and his heels should be slightly off the ground.
- The defender should be bent forward at the waist, his eyes and chest should be up, but his hips should be down.
- The player should have his arms relaxed, just below his knees.

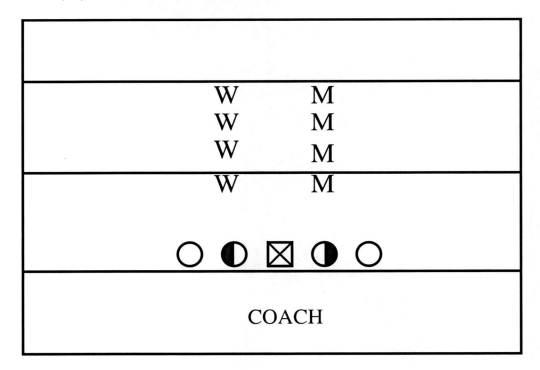

Drill #33: Key—Read Steps

Objective: To develop the linebacker's stance and read steps

Equipment Needed: Five tires

Description: Align the five tires on a yard line, one yard apart. The linebackers should align in two lines on the outside shoulder of the guard (30 technique). The coach should be in the fullback position. When the coach gives the command "stance," all the linebackers should get into their stance. The coach will move right or left; all the players will mirror his movement with three 45-degree angle six-inch steps. The players should hold their stance until given the "break" command. Repeat the drill for five or six repetitions.

Coaching Points:
- The linebacker should be in a good stance.
- The player's three read steps should be quick, but under control.
- The player should not cross his feet.
- The player should not have any false steps.
- The player should keep his hips low and back flat.

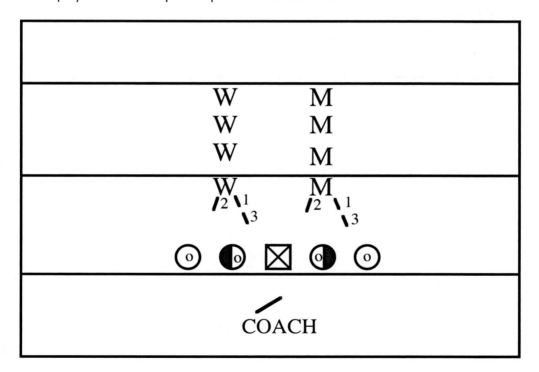

Drill #34: Key—Run Fits

Objective: To develop the linebacker's stance, read steps, and run fits

Equipment Needed: Five tires

Description: Align the five tires on a yard line, one yard apart. The linebackers should align in two lines on the outside shoulder of the guard (30 technique). The coach should be in the fullback position. When the coach gives the command "stance," all the linebackers should get into their stance. The coach will move right or left; the first player will mirror his movement with three 45-degree angle six-inch steps. The playside linebacker will continue to scrape to the C gap, and the backside linebacker will fill to the backside A gap. The players should hold their stance until given the "break" command. Repeat the drill for five or six repetitions.

Coaching Points:
- The linebacker should be in a good stance.
- The player's three read steps should be quick, but under control.
- The player should not cross his feet.
- The player should not have any false steps.
- The player should keep his hips low and back flat.
- The linebacker should move downhill to the line of scrimmage.
- Add fit and shuffle and read steps to counter fit.

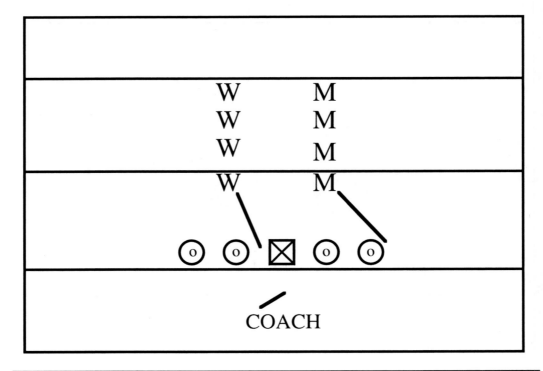

Drill #35: Key—Quick Game/Wide Screen

Objective: To develop the linebacker's stance, read steps, and quick game fits

Equipment Needed: Five tires

Description: Align the five tires on a yard line, one yard apart. The linebackers should align in two lines on the outside shoulder of the guard (30 technique). The coach should be in the quarterback position. When the coach gives the command "stance," all the linebackers should get into their stance. The coach will simulate a three-step drop and pass. On the coach's movement, the linebackers should execute their read steps. When they see wide quick game, the linebacker should plant his feet, pivot, turn to the direction the ball is thrown, and sprint to the ball. Repeat the drill for five or six repetitions.

Coaching Points:
- The linebacker should be in a good stance.
- The player should have three quick read steps, but under control.
- The player should not cross his feet.
- The player should not have any false steps.
- The player should keep his hips low and back flat.
- The player should pivot and turn to the direction the ball is thrown.

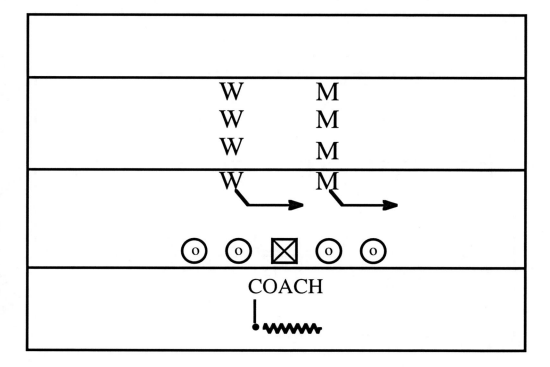

Drill #36: Key—Sprint-Out Pass

Objective: To develop the linebacker's stance, read steps, and sprint-out pass coverage

Equipment Needed: Five tires

Description: Align the five tires on a yard line, one yard apart. The linebackers should align in two lines on the outside shoulder of the guard (30 technique). The coach should be in the quarterback position. When the coach gives the command "stance," the first two linebackers should assume a proper stance. The coach will simulate a sprint-out pass action. On the coach's movement, the linebackers should execute their read steps. When they read sprint-out, the playside linebacker should scrape the C gap and spy the quarterback. The backside linebacker should plant his feet, pivot, turn to the direction of the sprint-out, and drive to the playside curl. Repeat the drill for five or six repetitions.

Coaching Points:
- The linebacker should be in a good stance.
- The player should have three quick read steps, but under control.
- The player should not cross his feet.
- The player should not have any false steps.
- The player should keep his hips low and back flat.

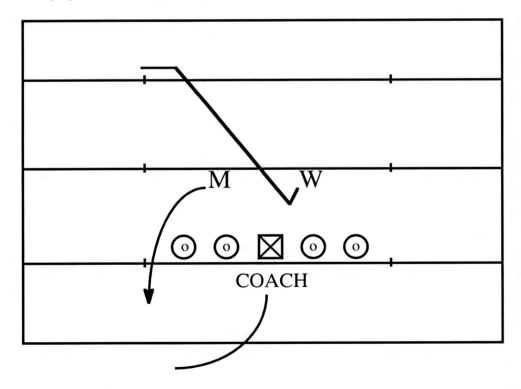

Drill #37: Key—Bootleg Pass

Objective: To develop the linebacker's stance, read steps, and bootleg pass coverage

Equipment Needed: Five tires

Description: Align the five tires on a yard line, one yard apart. The linebackers should align in two lines on the outside shoulder of the guard (30 technique). The coach should be in the quarterback position. When the coach gives the command "stance," the first two linebackers should assume a proper stance. The coach will simulate a bootleg pass action. On the coach's movement, the linebackers should execute their read steps. When they read bootleg, both linebackers should pivot and turn and drive to the opposite side curl. On the way to the curl, the linebacker should look over the downfield shoulder for the tight end crossing route. Repeat the drill for five or six repetitions.

Coaching Points:
- The linebacker should be in a good stance.
- The player should have three quick read steps, but under control.
- The player should not cross his feet.
- The player should not have any false steps.
- The player should pivot and drive to the opposite curl.

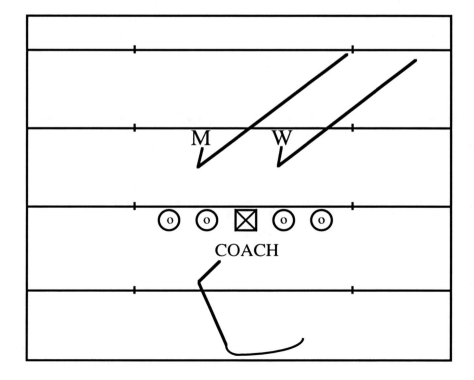

Drill #38: Key–Dropback Pass

Objective: To develop the linebacker's stance, read steps, and dropback pass coverage

Equipment Needed: Five tires

Description: Align the five tires on a yard line, one yard apart. The linebackers should align in two lines on the outside shoulder of the guard (30 technique). The coach should be in the quarterback position. When the coach gives the command "stance," the first two linebackers should assume a proper stance. The coach will simulate a dropback pass action. On the coach's movement, the linebackers should execute their read steps. When they read dropback, both linebackers should drop step, turn, and drive to the outside hook and slide to the curl, 10 to 12 yards deep. Repeat the drill for five or six repetitions.

Coaching Points:
- The linebacker should be in a good stance.
- The player should have three quick read steps, but under control.
- The player should not cross his feet.
- The player should not have any false steps.
- The player should have his head on a swivel looking from quarterback to receiver.

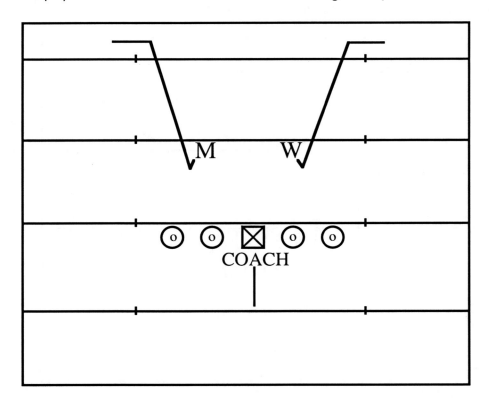

Drill #39: Defeating Blocks—Hand Shiver Progression

Objective: To develop the linebacker's ability to use the hand shiver technique to defeat a block

Equipment Needed: Two hand shields

Description: The two blockers align on a yard line, holding a shield. On the coach's command "stance," the players assume a proper stance, one foot from the blocker. On the whistle, the linebacker takes a six-inch jab step with his right foot, shooting his hands with his thumbs pointing up and striking the shield with the heels of his hands. The linebacker should lock his arms out and roll his hips. Execute five repetitions, and then step with the left foot. After all players have had their turn, repeat the drill from three steps away from the blocker and then five steps from the blocker.

Coaching Points:
- The defender should be in a good stance.
- The defender should take a six-inch power step and throw his hands at the shield.
- The defender should press and lock his arms out, as he is rolling his hips.
- The defender should hold this low position, buzzing his feet until the coach blows the whistle.

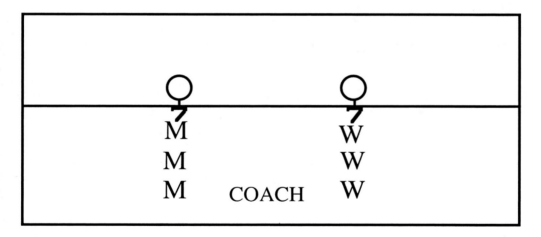

Drill #40: Defeating Blocks—Hand Shiver and Rip

Objective: To develop the linebacker's ability to use a hand shiver and rip technique to disengage from a blocker

Equipment Needed: None

Description: The two blockers align on a yard line, on the coach's command "fit," the defender assumes a proper three points of contact, hand shiver position. On the whistle, the linebacker should shimmy his feet, knocking the blocker back and simultaneously locking his arms out and rolling his hips. As the blocker is being knocked back, the defender should rip his left arm and leg past the blocker. Execute five repetitions, and then repeat ripping with the right arm. After all players have had their turn, repeat the drill from three steps away from the blocker and then five steps from the blocker.

Coaching Points:
- The defender should be in a good fit position.
- The defender should press and lock his arms out, as he is rolling his hips.
- The defender should execute a quick rip move.

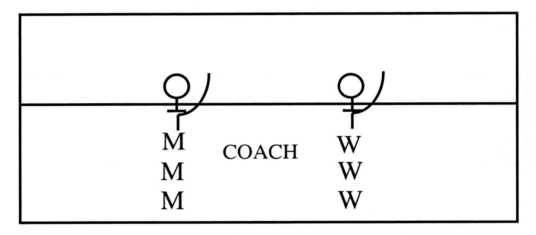

Drill #41: Defeating Blocks—Hand Shiver and Pull

Objective: To develop the linebacker's ability to use a hand shiver and pull technique to disengage from a blocker

Equipment Needed: None

Description: The two blockers align on a yard line, on the coach's command "fit," the defender assumes a proper three points of contact, hand shiver position. On the whistle, the linebacker should shimmy his feet, knocking the blocker back and simultaneously locking his arms out and rolling his hips. As the blocker is being knocked back, he should drop his hips. The defender should pull the blocker to the left and accelerate off the block. Execute five repetitions, and then repeat pulling the blocker to the right. After all players have had their turn, repeat the drill from three steps away from the blocker and then five steps from the blocker.

Coaching Points:
- The defender should be in a good fit position.
- The defender should press and lock his arms out, as he is rolling his hips.
- The defender should execute a quick pull move.

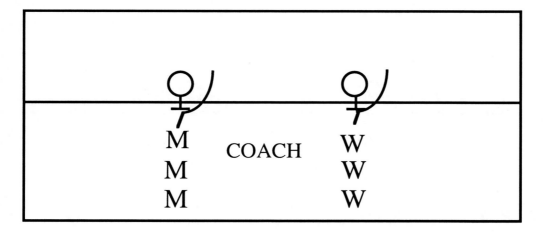

Drill #42: Defeating Blocks—Rip Progression

Objective: To develop the linebacker's ability to use the rip technique to defeat a block

Equipment Needed: Two hand shields

Description: The two blockers align on a yard line, holding a shield. On the coach's command "stance," the players assume a proper stance, one foot from the blocker. On the whistle, the linebacker takes a six-inch power step with his right foot, and then dipping his left shoulder while simultaneously ripping his left arm and leg through the block. Execute five repetitions, and then step with the left foot. After all players have had their turn, repeat the drill from three steps away from the blocker and then five steps from the blocker.

Coaching Points:
- The defender should be in a good stance.
- The defender should take a six-inch power step and dip and rip through the shield.
- The defender must clear through the blocker.
- The defender should hold this low ending position, buzzing his feet until the coach blows the whistle.

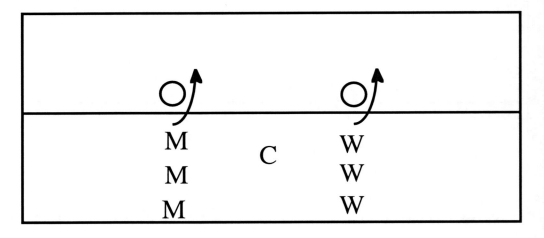

Drill #43: Defeating Blocks—Shoulder-Forearm Progression

Objective: To develop the linebacker's ability to use the shoulder-forearm technique to defeat a block

Equipment Needed: Two hand shields

Description: The two blockers align on a yard line, holding a shield. On the coach's command "stance," the players assume a proper stance, one foot from the blocker. On the whistle, the linebacker takes a six-inch power step with his right foot and then drives his left shoulder while simultaneously shooting the left forearm and leg toward the blocker. The defender's right hand should hand shiver and extend. Execute five repetitions and then step with the left foot. After all players have had their turn, repeat the drill from three steps away from the blocker and then five steps from the blocker.

Coaching Points:
- The defender should be in a good stance.
- The defender should take a six-inch power step and execute the shoulder-forearm technique into the shield.
- The defender must square up and squeeze the blocker to the inside and roll his hips.
- The defender should hold this low ending position, buzzing his feet until the coach blows the whistle.
- The thigh pad is the aiming point to defeat the block.

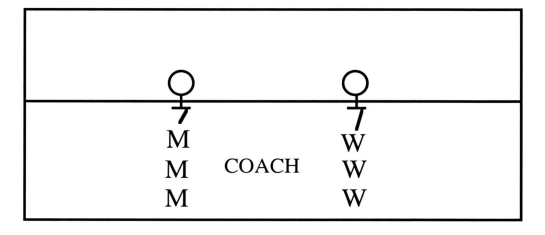

Drill #44: Man-to-Man Coverage Progression

Objective: To teach and develop the linebacker's ability to play man coverage

Equipment Needed: Three tires, two balls

Description: Align three tires on a yard line as the center, guard, and tackle. Place a running back behind the guard. The running back will run one of four routes (out, circle, bubble, or go). On the snap, the linebacker is reading the back, he should settle up and establish inside leverage and keep his eyes on the back's belt buckle. After the back has made his cut, the defender should eye the earhole of the back's helmet. This will let the defender know when the back is looking for the ball.

Coaching Points:

- Defending the out route, the defender should trail on the back's hip, watching the eye of the back. When defending the throw, he should break it up with the backfield arm, while keeps the downfield arm in a position to tackle (watching for out-and-up).
- Defending the circle route, the defender should wall the back. He should not allow the back to cross the field unchecked. He should not push off, and keep tight coverage.
- Defending the go route, the defender should keep inside leverage on the hip in a tight trail position.
- Defending the bubble route, the defender should close to the route as quickly as he can (watching for the wheel).
- The defender should not look away from the receiver for the ball until he has closed the gap and the receiver has his hands up and he is looking for the ball. This will allow the defender to play double moves.

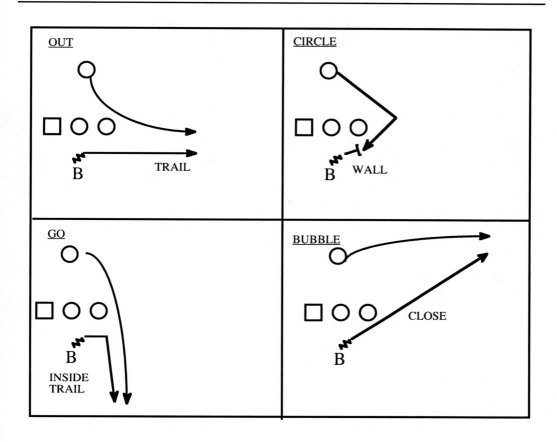

Drill #45: Cage

Objective: To teach linebackers how to attack and defeat blocks in a low position, using a rip, hand shiver, or shoulder-forearm technique

Equipment Needed: One cage (10′ wide x 10′ long x 4′6″ high), three hand shields.

Description: Have a group of blockers with the shields on one end of the cage and the linebackers on the other end of the cage. The first rotation should be the rip technique to the left and then to the right. Second is hand shiver, and third is shoulder-forearm. On the command "stance," one player on each end of the cage assumes a proper stance. When the coach blows the whistle, the linebacker takes his three read steps and moves through the cage and executes the proper technique to defeat the block.

Coaching Points:
- Executing the rip and hand shiver technique, align the linebacker on an offset angle to the blocker.
- Executing the shoulder-forearm technique, align the linebacker head-up on the blocker.
- Adding a ballcarrier to the drill is an option.

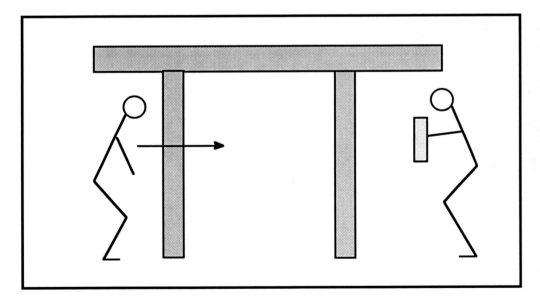

Drill #46: One-Man Sled

Objective: To develop the linebacker's ability to use the rip, hand shiver, and shoulder-forearm technique to defeat a block

Equipment Needed: A one-man sled

Description: The linebackers should get in a single file line. The first linebacker should assume a proper stance three yards from the sled. On the coach's whistle, the player will take three read steps and then attack the pad and execute the technique requested by the coach (rip/hand shiver/shoulder-forearm). Execute the drills to the right and the left.

Coaching Points:
- When executing the rip technique, the player should align three yards off and two steps to a side of the sled pad. The player read steps with the near foot and scrapes toward the sled, dipping and ripping the inside arm. After clearing the pad, the defender should shuffle out.
- When executing the shoulder-forearm technique, the player should align three yards off and head-up on the sled pad. On the whistle, the player should take his read steps and then attack the sled pad. On contact, the defender should fit his right shoulder and forearm and stab his left hand. The player should roll his hips and keep his feet running until the whistle sounds again.
- When executing the hand shiver technique, the player should align three yards off and two steps to the side of the sled pad. The player read steps with the near foot and fills toward the sled. The defender should make three points of contact, press and lock out his arms, roll his hips, and run his feet. The player should execute a disengage move (pull or rip). After the defender disengages past the sled, he should shuffle out.

5

Outside Linebacker Drills

Drill #47: Stance and Alignment—To an Open End

Objective: To teach and develop the outside linebacker's stance and alignment to the open end

Equipment Needed: Five tires

Description: Align the five tires on the yard line one yard apart. The outside linebackers should align in two lines, right and left outside linebackers, two yards from the offensive tackle on the line of scrimmage (ghost 6). On the command "stance," all the outside linebackers should get into their stance. The players should hold their stance until they are given the "break" command. Repeat the drill.

Coaching Points:
- The outside linebacker should have his feet slightly wider than shoulder-width apart, and his outside foot should be staggered back heel to toe.
- The defender's ankles and knees should be flexed.
- The defender should be bent at the waist. His eyes and chest should be up, but his hips should be down.
- The defender should have his arms relaxed, just below his knees.
- The defender should have his weight balanced.
- If the defender must widen to an apex alignment from the tackle to the #2 receiver, he has the same stance as a ghost 6 alignment. The alignment changes to half way out to #2 and five yards off the line of scrimmage.

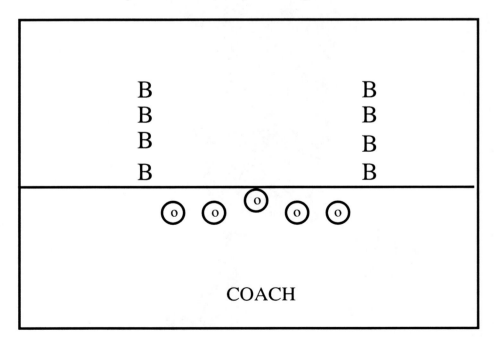

Drill #48: Stance and Alignment—On a Tight End

Objective: To teach and develop the outside linebacker's stance and alignment on a tight end

Equipment Needed: Five tires

Description: Align the five tires on the yard line one yard apart and two players in the tight end position. The outside linebackers should align in two lines: right and left outside linebackers. The outside linebacker should align on the line of scrimmage, with his inside shoulder aligned on the outside shoulder of the tight end (9 technique). On the command "stance," the first outside linebackers should get into their stance. The players should hold their stance until they are given the "break" command. Repeat the drill.

Coaching Points:
- The outside linebacker should have his feet slightly wider than shoulder-width apart, and his outside foot should be staggered back heel to toe.
- The defender's ankles and knees should be flexed.
- The defender should be bent at the waist with his chest over his thighs. His eyes should be up, but his hips should be down to where his back is flat.
- The defender should have his arms cocked, just above his knees ready to hand shiver the tight end.
- The defender should have his weight slightly forward.

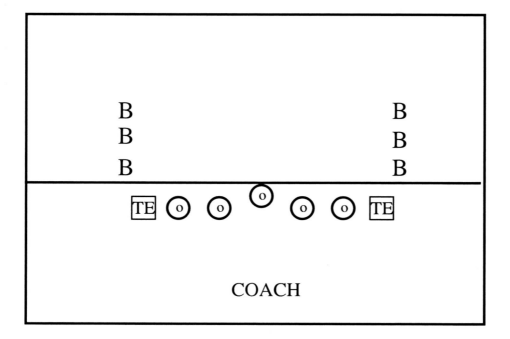

Drill # 49: Hand Shiver—Six-Point Progression

Objective: To develop the outside linebacker's ability to deliver a blow on a blocker

Equipment Needed: Two shields

Description: The players should face the shield aligned in an outside shade, in a six-point stance (toe's, knees, and hands) on the ground, coiled back six inches from the pad. On the whistle, the players should shoot their hands at the pad with their thumbs pointed up. The heels of their hand and mask should hit the pad, and they should press their arms out and roll their hips. Repeat for three repetitions, and switch groups. Then, move to a two- point-stance power step technique.

Coaching Points:
- The players should strike the pad with the heels of their hands and their thumbs pointing upward.
- The players should grab the pad and press.
- When the players perform the two-point explosion, their feet should keep chopping until the whistle blows.

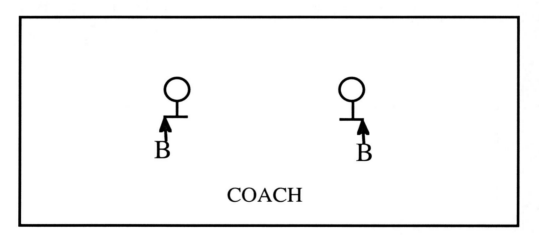

Drill #50: Defeating Blocks—Hand Shiver and Pull

Objective: To develop the outside linebacker's ability to use a hand shiver and pull technique to disengage from a blocker

Equipment Needed: None

Description: The two blockers align on a yard line. On the coach's command "fit," the defender assumes a proper three points of contact, hand shiver position. On the whistle, the outside linebacker should shimmy his feet, knocking the blocker back simultaneously locking his arms out and rolling his hips. As the blocker is being knocked back, he should drop his hips. The defender should pull the blocker to the left and accelerate off the block. Execute five repetitions, and then repeat, pulling the blocker to the right.

Coaching Points:
- The defender should be in a good fit position.
- The defender should press and lock his arms out, as he is rolling his hips and buzzing his feet.
- The defender should execute a quick pull move and accelerate off the block toward the ball location.

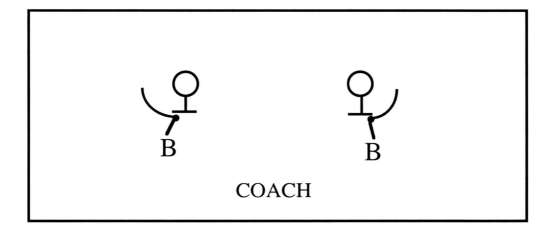

Drill #51: Defeating Blocks—Hand Shiver and Rip

Objective: To develop the outside linebacker's ability to use a hand shiver and rip technique to disengage from a blocker

Equipment Needed: None

Description: The two blockers align on a yard line. On the coach's command "fit," the defender assumes a proper three points of contact, hand shiver position. On the whistle, the outside linebacker should shimmy his feet, knocking the blocker back simultaneously locking his arms out and rolling his hips. As the blocker is being knocked back, the defender should rip through the blocker to the left and accelerate off the block. Execute five repetitions, and then repeat, ripping through the blocker to the right.

Coaching Points:
- The defender should be in a good fit position.
- The defender should press and lock his arms out, as he is rolling his hips and buzzing his feet.
- The defender should execute a quick rip move and accelerate off the block toward the ball location.

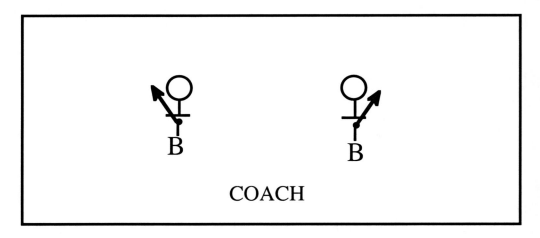

Drill #52: 1-on-1 Reach and Base Block

Objective: To develop the outside linebacker's technique to defeat the reach and base blocks of the tight end

Equipment Needed: None

Description: The outside linebackers align by position in two groups five yards apart. The coach hand signals to the blocker which direction to simulate the block. On the whistle, the two blockers simulate the block. On the blocker's movement, the outside linebacker should power-step with the playside foot, attack the blocker, and hand shiver him. The linebacker should keep fighting pressure and press and lock out the blocker. He should continue to fight down the line and disengage with a push-pull or rip move. Rotate the groups, and repeat the drill.

Coaching Points:
- The defenders should power-step and hand shiver the blocker.
- The defenders should keep their feet driving on contact, roll their hips, and lock their arms out.
- The defenders should attack the blocker.

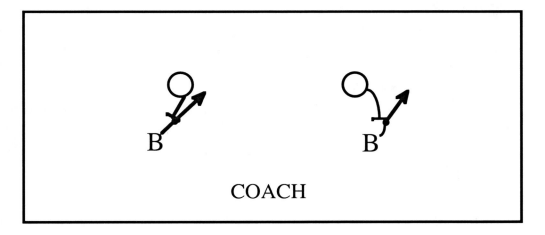

Drill #53: Down and Kick (Fullback or Guard)

Objective: To develop the outside linebacker's ability to play the tight end down block and fullback or guard kick-out

Equipment Needed: Two hand shields, two tires

Description: Align a tight end on a yard line with an outside linebacker aligned in a 9 technique. Also, align a blocker with a shield in the fullback position and another blocker with a shield in the near side guard position. Align one tire as the tackle and one as the center. The tight end is blocking down every play. The coach will point to the fullback or the guard, indicating which one is the kick-out blocker, and give a snap count. On the snap, the outside linebacker should read the down block of the tight end. He should power-step inside and hand shiver the tight end, shuffle his feet, and squeeze him down. While he is squeezing the tight end, the defender should be looking through the hip of the tight end into the backfield. The defender is looking to hit the next thing that shows. When the outside linebacker sees either the fullback or the guard coming to kick him out, he should attack the blocker with his outside shoulder and forearm. On contact, he should drive his feet and wheel upfield. Repeat the drill several times, and then run the drill from the other side.

Coaching Points:
- The defender should be in a good stance.
- The defender should get a good inside power step when the tight end blocks down.
- The defender must not take false steps.
- The defender must stay low during the entire drill.
- The defender's aiming point on the wrong arm must be the inside thigh pad of the blocker.

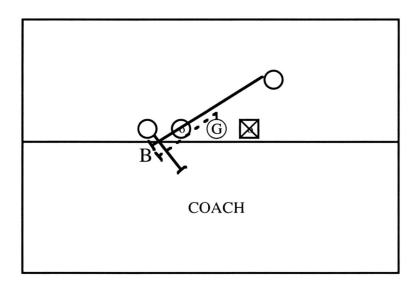

Drill #54: Down and Log (Fullback or Guard)

Objective: To develop the outside linebacker's ability to play the tight end down block and fullback or guard log block

Equipment Needed: Two hand shields, two tires

Description: Align a tight end on a yard line with an outside linebacker aligned in a 9 technique. Also align a blocker with a shield in the fullback position and another blocker with a shield in the near side guard position. Align one tire as the tackle and one as the center. The tight end is blocking down every play. The coach will point to the fullback or the guard, indicating which one is the blocker and give a snap count. On the snap, the outside linebacker should read the down block of the tight end. He should power-step inside and hand shiver the tight end, shuffle his feet, and squeeze him down. While he is squeezing the tight end, the defender should be looking through the hip of the tight end in to the backfield. The defender is looking to hit the next thing that shows. When the outside linebacker sees either the fullback or the guard moving toward on an angle, trying to cross his face, he should redirect and attack the blocker's outside shoulder with an explosive hand shiver. On contact, he should drive his feet and push-pull or rip upfield. Repeat the drill several times, and then run the drill from the other side.

Coaching Points:
- The defender should be in a good stance.
- The defender should get a good inside power step when the tight end blocks down.
- The defender must not take false steps.
- The defender must stay low during the entire drill.
- The defender's aiming point versus the log block must be the outside pad of the blocker.

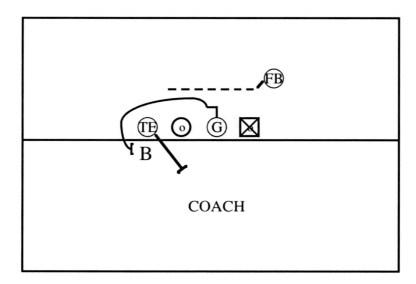

Drill #55: Option Slow Play

Objective: To develop the outside linebacker's ability to defend the dive option play to the tight end arc release

Equipment Needed: None

Description: Align one player in the tight end position, one as a quarterback, and one as a fullback. On the snap, the tight end should arc release, and the quarterback and fullback should simulate a dive option action. The outside linebacker should power-step with his outside foot and hand shiver the tight end, and play the reach block, forcing the tight end wide. When the defender recognizes the tight end is arc releasing, he should settle off the line of scrimmage and get his eyes back inside. When the defender recognizes the dive option and the quarterback is attacking the perimeter, he should slowly shuffle wider. Do not force the quarterback to pitch the ball. If the quarterback tucks the ball and turns upfield, the defender should cross over and make the tackle. If the quarterback pitches the ball, the defender should turn and run down the line to the pitch. Repeat the drill on the other side.

Coaching Points:
- The defender should be in a good stance.
- The defender should get a good outside power step when the tight end arcs.
- The defender must not cross the line of scrimmage.
- The defender must stay low during the entire drill.
- The defender slow-plays the quarterback to buy time for pursuit.

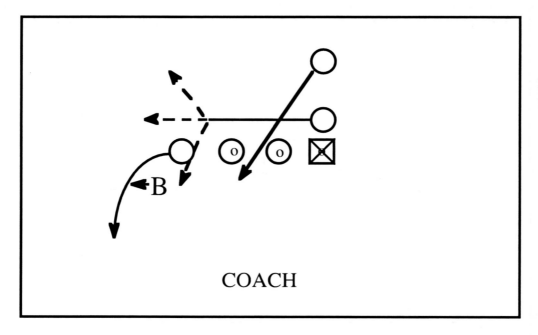

COACH

Drill #56: Speed Rush

Objective: To develop the outside linebacker's ability to pass rush, using a speed rush technique

Equipment Needed: One stand-up dummy, three tires, two hand shields

Description: Place the three tires on a yard line one yard apart, as the center and two guards. Place the dummy seven yards deep behind the center. Align two players each with a hand shield in the offensive tackle position. The outside linebacker should align in a ghost 6 alignment. On the snap, the blocker should pass set, and the defender should accelerate upfield. As the defender closes on the blocker, he should attack the outside half of the blocker with a quick dip and rip his inside arm and shoulder. As the defender makes contact, he should lean into the blocker and squeeze to the quarterback. Alternately, the left outside linebacker goes, and the right outside linebacker goes.

Coaching Points:
- The defender should start in a good stance.
- The defender should read the tackle and move on his movement.
- The defender must explode upfield and commit to beating the tackle with speed around the corner.
- The defender should use his outside arm to chop or lift the outside arm of the blocker.

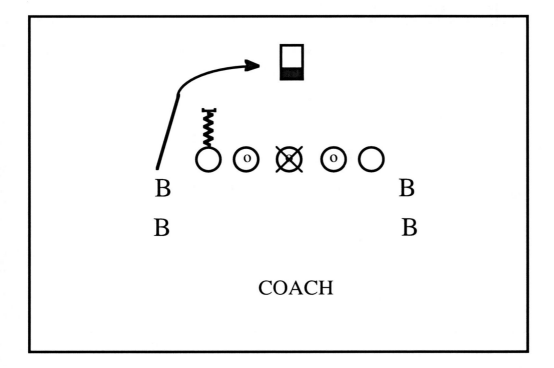

Drill #57: Speed Rush to Power Rush Counter

Objective: To develop the outside linebacker's ability to pass rush, using a speed rush to power rush counter, when the tackle turns his shoulders during his pass set

Equipment Needed: One stand-up dummy, three tires, two hand shields

Description: Place the three tires on a yard line one yard apart, as the center and two guards. Place the dummy seven yards deep behind the center. Align two players each with a hand shield in the offensive tackle position. The outside linebacker should align in a ghost 6 alignment. On the snap, the blocker will pass set. On his third step, he should turn his shoulders to the outside. The defender should accelerate upfield. As the defender closes on the blocker and sees the tackle turn his shoulders, he should attack the middle of the blocker, hand shivering the blocker with a quick power move. As the defender makes contact, he should lean into the blocker and drive him back to the quarterback. Alternately, the left outside linebacker goes, and the right outside linebacker goes.

Coaching Points:
- The defender should start in a good stance.
- The defender should read the tackle and move on his movement.
- The defender must explode upfield and commit to beating the tackle with speed around the corner.
- When the defender sees the tackle turning his shoulders, he should then counter to the power rush.

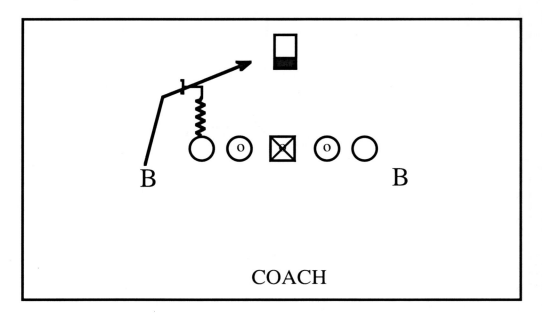

Drill #58: Speed Rush and Spin Counter

Objective: To develop the outside linebacker's ability to pass rush, using a speed rush and spin counter technique when he has rushed deeper than the quarterback's drop

Equipment Needed: One stand-up dummy, three tires, two hand shields

Description: Place the three tires on a yard line one yard apart, as the center and two guards. Place the dummy seven yards deep behind the center. Align two players each with a hand shield in the offensive tackle position. The outside linebacker should align in a ghost 6 alignment. On the snap, the blocker should pass set, and the defender should accelerate upfield. As the defender closes on the blocker, he should attack the outside half of the blocker with a quick dip and rip his inside arm and shoulder. As the defender makes contact, he should lean into the blocker and squeeze to the quarterback. As he sees he is deeper in the backfield than the quarterback, he should drop his hips and spin inside quickly. Alternately, the left outside linebacker goes, and then the right outside linebacker goes.

Coaching Points:
- The defender should start in a good stance.
- The defender should read the tackle and move on his movement.
- The defender must explode upfield and commit to beating the tackle with speed around the corner.
- The defender must not spin inside too early, or he will lose rush contain.
- When the defender spins, it must be quick and tight to the blocker.
- The defender should whip his outside arm around and seal the blocker, and then accelerate off the block to the quarterback.

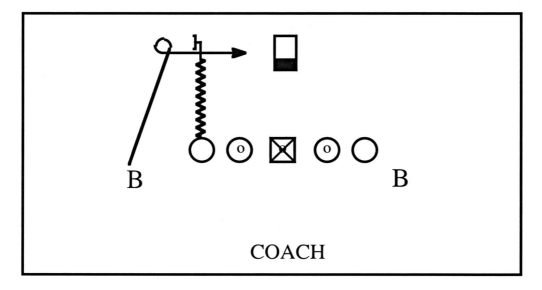

Drill #59: Pass Rush vs. the Back

Objective: To develop the outside linebacker's ability to pass rush 1-on-1 against a back

Equipment Needed: One stand up dummy, five tires, two hand shields

Description: Place the five tires on a yard line one yard apart. Place the dummy seven yards deep behind the center. Align two players each with a hand shield in the halfback position. The outside linebacker should align in a ghost 6 alignment. On the snap, the blocker should settle up to pass protect, and the defender should accelerate upfield. As the defender closes on the blocker, he should attack the outside half of the blocker with a power rush move. As the defender makes contact, he should lean into the blocker and drive the blocker back to the quarterback. Alternately, the left outside linebacker goes, and the right outside linebacker goes.

Coaching Points:
- The defender should start in a good stance.
- The defender should read the back and move on his movement.
- The defender must explode upfield.
- The defender should use a quick pull move, if he feels the blocker leaning forward.

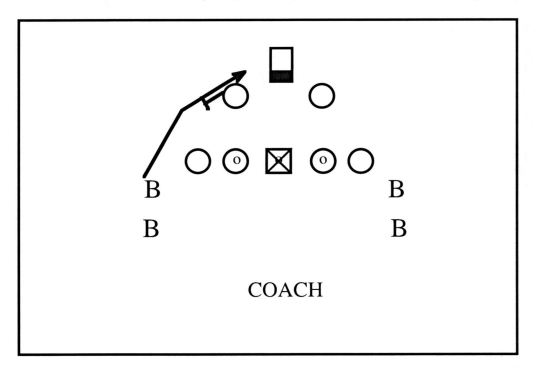

Drill #60: Curl Drop Progression #1

Objective: To develop the outside linebacker's ability to pattern read the #2 receiver and to defend the vertical release by the #2 receiver

Equipment Needed: Three tires

Description: Align the three tires on a yard line as the center, guard, and tackle. Align a player as the quarterback and two as wide receivers. Align an outside linebacker 4 x 5 yards off the #2 receiver. On the snap, the quarterback should take a five-step drop, the #2 receiver should run a seam route, and the #1 receiver should run a five-yard stop route. The outside linebacker should take his read steps as he is reading his key. During his read steps, the defender should see the quarterback taking a five-step drop. The defender should the find the #2 receiver, widen toward the receiver, but keep inside leverage. The outside linebacker should push and reroute the receiver, and then settle to 12 to 14 yards, seeing the #1 receiver, but staying in the throwing lane of the seam route. Repeat the drill, and then run the drill on the other side.

Coaching Points:
- The defender should be in a good stance, reading the quarterback as his key.
- The defender should find and open up to the #2 receiver.
- The defender should reroute the receiver and wall him to the outside.
- After the defender has carried the receiver to 12 to 14 yards deep, he should square up to the line of scrimmage as he finds the #1 receiver and stays under and inside the seam route of #2.

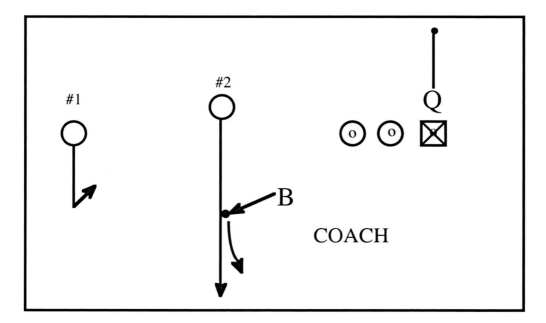

Drill #61: Curl Drop Progression #2

Objective: To develop the outside linebacker's ability to pattern read the #2 receiver and to defend the outside release by the #2 receiver and curl route by #1 receiver

Equipment Needed: Three tires

Description: Align the three tires on a yard line as the center, guard, and tackle. Align a player as the quarterback and two as wide receivers. Align an outside linebacker 4 x 5 yards off the #2 receiver. On the snap, the quarterback should take a five-step drop, the #2 receiver should run a five-yard out route, and the #1 receiver should run a 12-yard curl route. The outside linebacker should take his read steps as he is reading his key. During his read steps, the defender should see the quarterback taking a five-step drop. The defender should open to and find the #2 receiver. When he sees #2 running an out route, he should begin to drop to the curl area and locate the #1 receiver. When he sees #1 running a curl, he should move to he getting inside and underneath #1. Repeat the drill, and then run the drill on the other side.

Coaching Points:
- The defender should be in a good stance, reading the quarterback as his key.
- The defender should find and open up to the #2 receiver.
- The defender should not chase #2 but locate #1 and defend the curl route.
- The defender should wall #1, do not allow him to get to the inside.

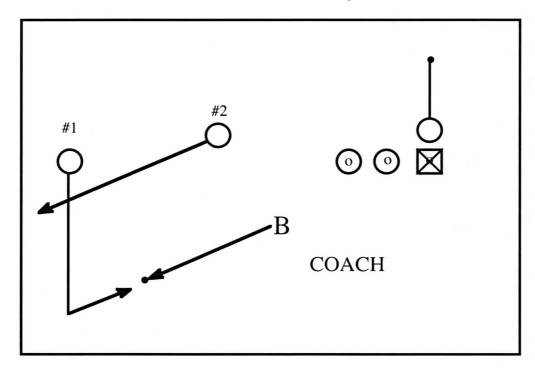

Drill #62: Curl Drop Progression #3

Objective: To develop the outside linebacker's ability to pattern read the #2 receiver and to defend the inside release by the #2 receiver and dig route by the #1 receiver

Equipment Needed: Three tires

Description: Align the three tires on a yard line as the center, guard, and tackle. Align a player as the quarterback and two as wide receivers. Align an outside linebacker 4 x 5 yards off the #2 receiver. On the snap, the quarterback should take a five-step drop, the #2 receiver should run a shallow cross route, and the #1 receiver should run a 12-yard dig route. The outside linebacker should take his read steps as he is reading his key. During his read steps, the defender should see the quarterback taking a five-step drop. The defender should open to and find the #2 receiver. When he sees #2 running a shallow cross route, he should try to reroute the receiver and then to drop to the curl area and locate the #1 receiver. When he sees #1 running a dig, he should move toward the dig route, getting inside and underneath #1 receiver. Repeat the drill, and then run the drill on the other side.

Coaching Points:
- The defender should be in a good stance, reading the quarterback as his key.
- The defender should find and open up to the #2 receiver.
- The defender should not chase #2, but locate but reroute him, and then locate #1 and drop to the dig route.
- The defender should wall #1, and not allow him to get to the inside.
- If the #1 receiver gets inside the outside linebacker, he should pivot and make a zone turn to the inside and run with him.

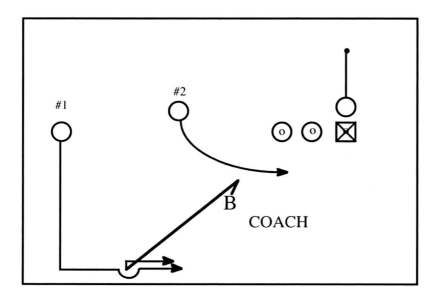

Drill #63: Zone Block vs. the Tackle

Objective: To develop the outside linebacker's technique to defeat the zone block of the tackle

Equipment Needed: None

Description: The outside linebackers align by position in two groups five yards apart. On the whistle, the two blockers simulate the zone block. On the blockers' movement, the outside linebacker should power-step with the outside foot, attack the blocker, and hand shiver him. The linebacker should keep fighting pressure and press and lock out the blocker. He should continue to fight down the line and disengage with a push-pull or rip move. Rotate the groups, and repeat the drill.

Coaching Points:
- The defender should power-step and hand shiver the blocker.
- The defender should keep his feet driving on contact, roll his hips, and lock his arms out.
- The defender should attack the blocker and keep his head on the outside pad of the tackle.
- The defender should push and pull and disengage off the block and set the edge.

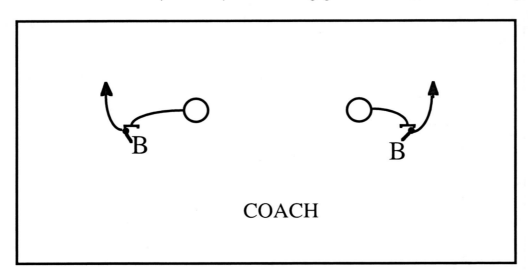

Drill #64: Fan Block vs. the Tackle

Objective: To develop the outside linebacker's technique to defeat the fan block of the tackle

Equipment Needed: None

Description: The outside linebackers align by position in two groups five yards apart. On the whistle, the two blockers simulate the fan block. On the blockers' movement, the outside linebacker should power-step with the inside foot, attack the blocker, and hand shiver him. The linebacker should keep fighting pressure and press and lock out the blocker. He should continue to fight and squeeze down the line and disengage with a push-pull or rip move across the face of the blocker. Rotate the groups, and repeat the drill.

Coaching Points:
- The defender should power-step and hand shiver the blocker.
- The defender should keep his feet driving on contact, roll his hips, and lock his arms out.
- The defender should attack the blocker and keep his head outside.
- The defender should not come upfield.
- The defender should keep his shoulders and the blocker's shoulders square to the line of scrimmage.
- The defender should push and pull and disengage across the blocker's face.

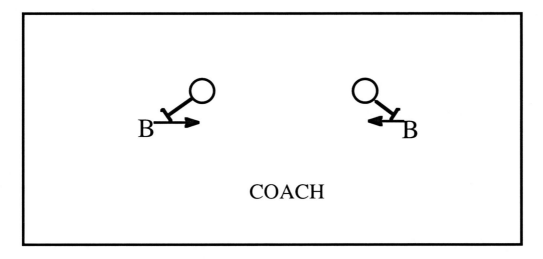

6

Defensive Back Drills

Drill #65: Pedal and Break Forward

Objective: To develop the defensive backs' stance and backpedal

Equipment Needed: Four cones, five balls

Description: Place the four cones on the yard line five yards apart. The first group of defensive backs should align in front of the cone. On the command "stance," the four defenders should assume a proper stance. He should have a narrow base, inside foot up, heel to toe, and ankles, knees, and waist bent. On the "go" command (coach moves the ball up), the defensive back should begin a controlled backpedal. On ball movement down, the defender should plant and drive forward, and the next player waiting in line throws a ball to him. The defender catches the ball, tucks it away, yells "Oskie," and runs past the cone. Switch groups, and repeat the drill.

Coaching Points:
- The defenders should be in a good stance.
- The defenders should use a controlled backpedal.
- The defenders should stick and drive off the plant foot.
- The defenders should look the ball in and catch it with two hands.

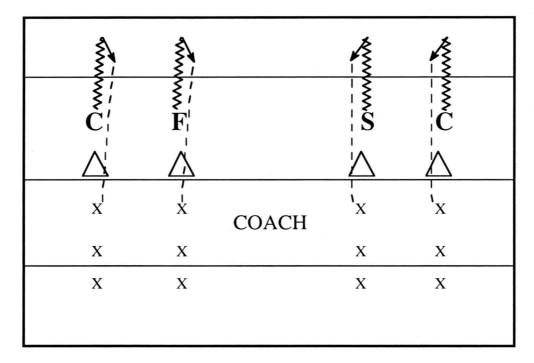

Drill #66: Pedal and Break 45

Objective: To develop the defensive backs' stance, backpedal, and 45-degree-angle break

Equipment Needed: Four cones, five balls

Description: Place the four cones on the yard line five yards apart. The first group of defensive backs should align in front of the cone. On the command "stance," the four defenders should assume a proper stance. He should have a narrow base, inside foot up, heel to toe, and ankles, knees, and waist bent. On the "go" command (coach moves the ball up), the defensive back should begin a controlled backpedal. On ball movement down and to the right, the defenders should plant and drive forward on a 45-degree angle, and the next player waiting in line throws a ball to him. The defender catches the ball, tucks it away, yells "Oskie," and runs past the cone. Switch groups, and repeat the drill.

Coaching Points:
- The defenders should be in a good stance.
- The defenders should use a controlled backpedal.
- The defenders should stick and drive off the plant foot.
- The defenders should look the ball in and catch it with two hands.

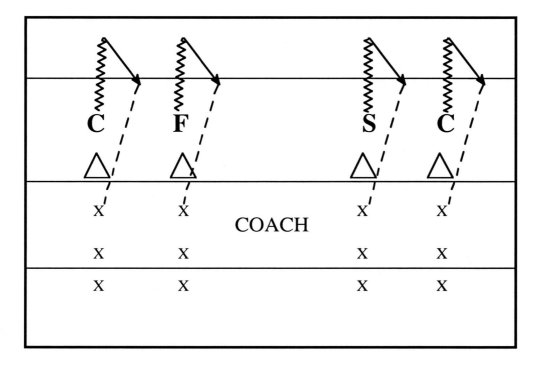

Drill #67: Pedal and Break 125

Objective: To develop the defensive backs' stance, backpedal, and post and corner angle break

Equipment Needed: Four cones, five balls

Description: Place the four cones on the yard line five yards apart. The first group of defensive backs should align in front of the cone. On the command "stance," the four defenders should assume a proper stance. He should have a narrow base, inside foot up, heel to toe, and ankles, knees, and waist bent. On the "go" command (coach moves the ball up), the defensive back should begin a controlled backpedal. On ball movement up and to the right, the defenders should open their hips on a 125-degree angle (post or corner route), and the next player waiting in line throws a ball to him. The defender catches the ball, tucks it away, yells "Oskie," and runs past the cone. Switch groups, and repeat the drill.

Coaching Points:
- The defenders should be in a good stance.
- The defenders should use a controlled backpedal.
- The defenders should open their hips and drive off the plant foot to the ball.
- The defenders should look the ball in and catch it with two hands.

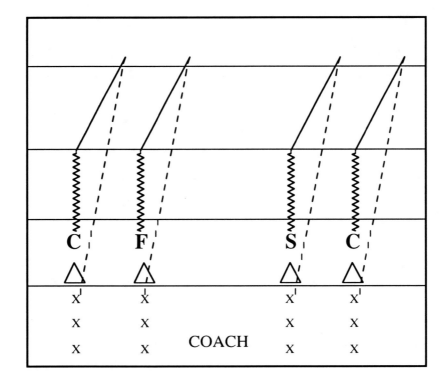

Drill #68: Pedal and Break 180

Objective: To develop the defensive backs' stance, backpedal, and defending the go

Equipment Needed: Four cones, five balls

Description: Place the four cones on the yard line five yards apart. The first group of defensive backs should align in front of the cone. On the command "stance," the four defenders should assume a proper stance. He should have a narrow base, inside foot up, heel to toe, and ankles, knees, and waist bent. On the "go" command (coach moves the ball up), the defensive back should begin a controlled backpedal. On ball movement up and over the head, the defenders should open their hips on a 180-degree angle (go route), and the next player waiting in line throws a ball to him. The defender catches the ball, tucks it away, yells "Oskie," and runs past the cone. Switch groups, and repeat the drill.

Coaching Points:
- The defenders should be in a good stance.
- The defenders should use a controlled backpedal.
- The defenders should open their hips and drive off the plant foot to the ball.
- The defenders should look the ball in and catch it with two hands.

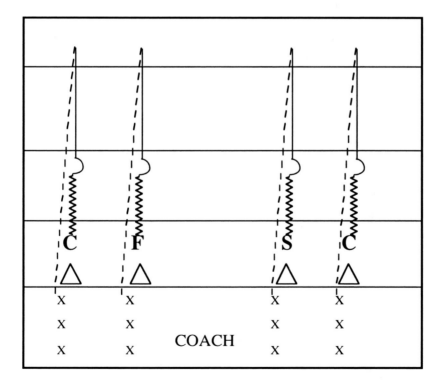

Drill #69: Pedal and Break 125 to Speed Turn

Objective: To develop the defensive backs' ability to defend the post corner

Equipment Needed: Four cones, five balls

Description: Place the four cones on the yard line five yards apart. The first group of defensive backs should align in front of the cone. On the command "stance," the four defenders should assume a proper stance. He should have a narrow base, inside foot up, heel to toe, and ankles, knees, and waist bent. On the "go" command (coach moves the ball up), the defensive back should begin a controlled backpedal. On the coach's shoulder movement left, the defenders should open their hips on a 125-degree angle to the right. On the coach's second shoulder move, the defender should speed turn, whipping his head and shoulders around to defend the double move. On the speed turn, the next player waiting in line throws a ball to him. The defender catches the ball, tucks it away, yells "Oskie," and runs past the cone. Switch groups, and repeat the drill.

Coaching Points:
- The defenders should be in a good stance.
- The defenders should use a controlled backpedal.
- The defenders should roll off the inside foot and drive to the ball.
- The defenders should look the ball in and catch it with two hands.

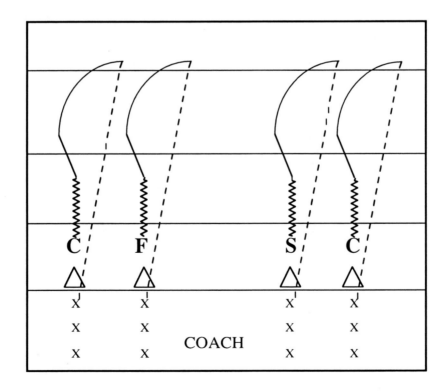

Drill #70: Shuffle and Break

Objective: To develop the defensive backs' stance and shuffle technique

Equipment Needed: Four cones, five balls

Description: Place the four cones on the yard line five yards apart. The first group of defensive backs should align in front of the cone. On the command "stance," the four defenders should assume a proper stance. He should have a narrow base, outside foot up, heel to toe, and ankles, knees, and waist bent. On the "go" command (coach moves the ball up), the defensive back should begin a controlled shuffle. He should step with his back foot and slightly drag his front foot. On ball movement down, the defender should plant and drive forward, and the next player waiting in line throws a ball to him. The defender catches the ball, tucks it away, yells "Oskie," and runs past the cone. Switch groups, and repeat the drill.

Coaching Points:
- The defenders should be in a good stance.
- The defenders should use a controlled shuffle technique.
- The defenders should stick and drive off the plant foot.
- The defenders should look the ball in and catch it with two hands.
- The coach should change the break to 45 degrees, 90 degrees, 125 degrees, 180 degrees

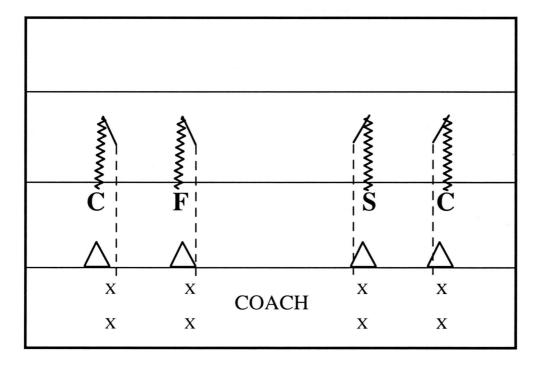

Drill #71: Mirror

Objective: To develop man-to-man coverage and concentration

Equipment Needed: None

Description: Place four offensive players on the sideline five yards apart. Align the four defensive backs on the inside shoulder and three yards in front of and facing the receiver. On the start command, the receiver will run a weave pattern down the yard line. The defender will begin to backpedal and mirror the receiver, always staying on his inside shoulder.

Coaching Points:
- The defender should be in a good stance.
- The receiver should not weave wider than three yards.
- The defender should keep his shoulders square and weave his hips.
- The defender should stay in a low pedal.
- The defender should not cross his feet.

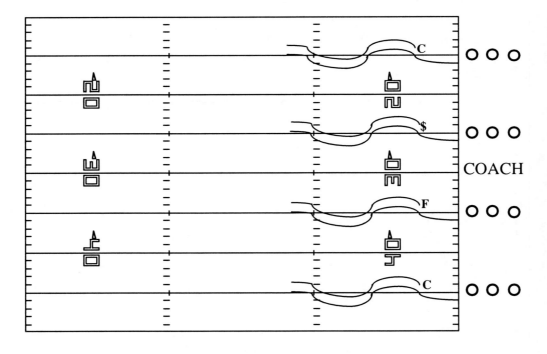

Drill #72: Rip the Stalk Block

Objective: To develop the defensive backs' ability to defeat the stalk block

Equipment Needed: Four cones, one ball, four hand shields.

Description: Place the four cones on the yard line five yards apart. The first group of defensive backs should align in front of the cone. On the command "stance," the four defenders should assume a proper stance. On the "go" command (coach moves the ball up), the defensive back should begin a controlled backpedal. On ball movement down, the defender should plant and drive forward, and the next player waiting in line should run at the defender and execute a stalk block. When the defender gets to the blocker, he should dip his right shoulder and rip his right arm through the pad the blocker is holding. Switch groups, and repeat the drill.

Coaching Points:
- The defenders should be in a good stance.
- The defenders should use a controlled backpedal.
- The defenders should stick and drive off the plant foot.
- The defenders should dip, rip, and accelerate through the block.

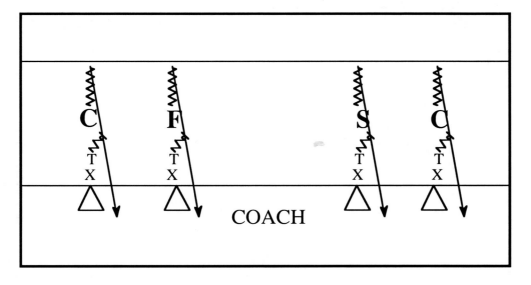

Drill #73: Set the Corner

Objective: To develop the defensive backs' ability to defeat the kick-out block of a guard or fullback

Equipment Needed: Three cones, two hand shields

Description: Place the three cones in a triangle five yards apart. The first two defensive backs should align to the side of their start cone. On the command "stance," the two defenders should assume a proper stance. On the "go" command, the defensive back should begin a controlled shuffle read. On the third shuffle step, the defender should plant and drive toward the blocker. The blocker should run at the defender and execute a kick-out block. When the defender gets to the blocker, he should dip his inside shoulder and attack the blocker with a shoulder-forearm technique. Switch groups, and repeat the drill.

Coaching Points:
- The defenders should be in a good stance.
- The defenders should use a controlled shuffle and stay low.
- The defenders should stick and drive off the plant foot.
- The defenders should attack the blocker.
- The defender should stay square to the line of scrimmage and keep his outside arm free.

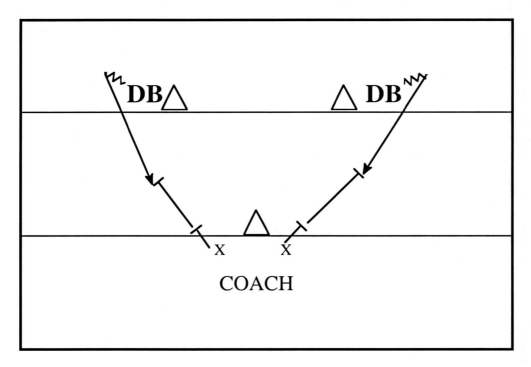

Drill #74: W

Objective: To develop the defensive backs' ability to backpedal plant and redirect

Equipment Needed: Five cones, three balls

Description: Place the five cones in the shape of a W five yards apart. The first group of defensive backs should align next to the first cone. On the command "stance," the defender should assume a proper stance. On the "go" command, the defensive back should begin a controlled backpedal. When the defender passes the second cone, he should plant and drive on an angle to the third cone, planting and backpedaling past the fourth cone. When he passes the fourth cone, he should plant and drive past the last cone. The coach should throw the ball to him as he gets to the last cone. The defender catches the ball, tucks it away, yells "Oskie," and runs past the cone. Switch groups, and repeat the drill.

Coaching Points:
- The defenders should be in a good stance.
- The defenders should use a controlled backpedal.
- The defenders should stick and drive off the plant foot.
- The defenders should look the ball in and catch it with two hands.

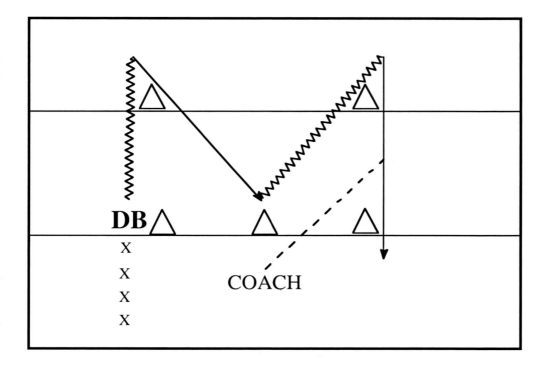

Drill #75: T-Step

Objective: To develop the defensive back's ability to backpedal and redirect, using the T-step technique

Equipment Needed: Four cones

Description: Place the four cones on the yard line five yards apart. The first group of defensive backs should align in front of the cone. On the command "stance," the four defenders should assume a proper stance. On the "go" command (coach moves the ball up), the defensive back should begin a controlled backpedal. On ball movement down, the defender should plant his left foot on an angle and place his right foot to form a "T" and drive forward, pushing off his back foot. Switch groups, and repeat the drill.

Coaching Points:
- The defenders should be in a good stance.
- The defenders should use a controlled backpedal.
- The defenders should stick and drive off the plant foot.
- The defenders should use his upper body to drive forward with his T-step.

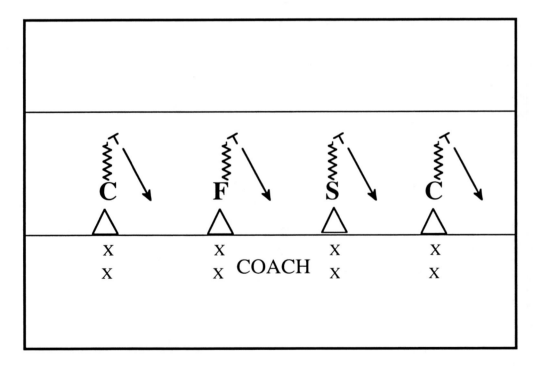

Drill #76: Break to the Ball

Objective: To emphasize to the defensive backs to drive back to the ball

Equipment Needed: Three balls

Description: Align all the defensive backs in one straight line on the hash, facing the sideline. The coach should stand on the sideline, and on his command, the first player in line should run toward the coach. As the player approaches the sideline, the coach should throw the ball to him. The player should catch the ball, tuck it away, and yell "Oskie." Repeat the drill until all the players execute a repetition.

Coaching Points:
- The defender should run full speed toward the coach.
- The defender should look the ball into his hands and tuck it away.

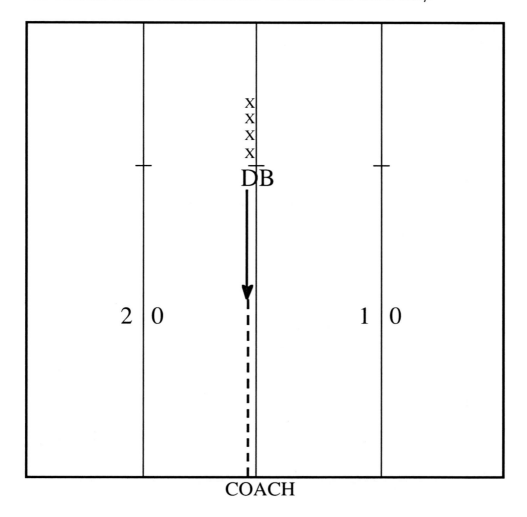

Drill #77: Break to the Ball 45 Degrees

Objective: To emphasize to the defensive backs to drive back to the ball on a 45-degree angle

Equipment Needed: Three balls

Description: Align all the defensive backs in one straight line on the hash, facing the sideline. The coach should stand on the sideline, and on his command, the first player in line should run toward the coach. As the player approaches the sideline, the coach should turn his shoulders to the right and then throw the ball. The player should break on a 45-degree angle when the coach turns his shoulders, catch the ball, tuck it away, and yell "Oskie." Repeat the drill until all the players execute a repetition. Then, repeat to the left.

Coaching Points:
- The defender should run full speed toward the coach.
- The defender should break on a 45-degree angle.
- The defender should look the ball into his hands and tuck it away.

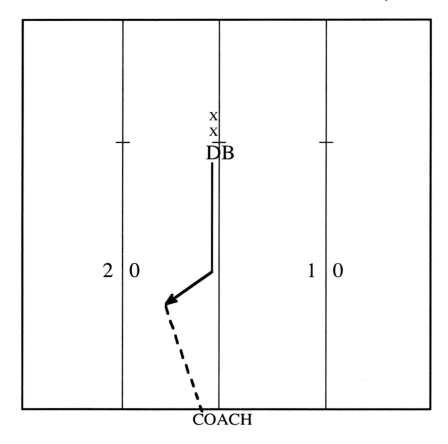

Drill #78: High Point

Objective: To emphasize to the defensive backs to drive back to the ball and catch it at its high point

Equipment Needed: Three balls

Description: Align all the defensive backs in one straight line on the hash, facing the sideline. The coach should stand on the sideline, and on his command, the first player in line should run toward the coach. As the player approaches the sideline, the coach should under hand lob the ball up into the air. The player should jump up into the air and catch the ball at the highest point he can, tuck it away, and yell "Oskie." Repeat the drill until all the players execute a repetition.

Coaching Points:
- The defender should run full speed toward the coach.
- The defender should catch the ball at a high point.
- The defender should look the ball into his hands and tuck it away.

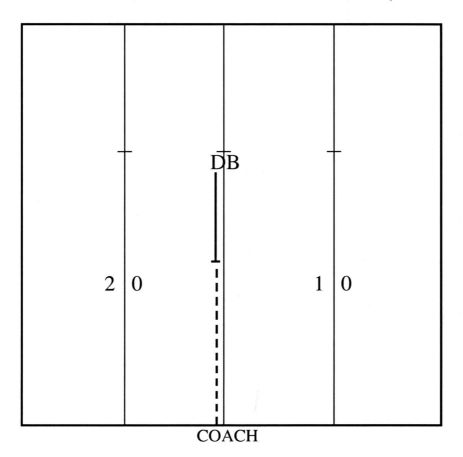

Drill #79: Tipped Ball

Objective: To emphasize to the defensive backs to drive back to the ball and improve their eye-hand coordination

Equipment Needed: Three balls

Description: Align all the defensive backs in one straight line on the hash, facing the sideline. The coach should stand on the sideline, and on his command, the first player in line should run toward the coach. As the player approaches the sideline, the coach should throw a bad ball to him. The player should catch the ball, tuck it away, and yell "Oskie." Repeat the drill until all the players execute a repetition.

Coaching Points:
- The defender should run full speed toward the coach.
- The defender should look the ball into his hands and tuck it away.

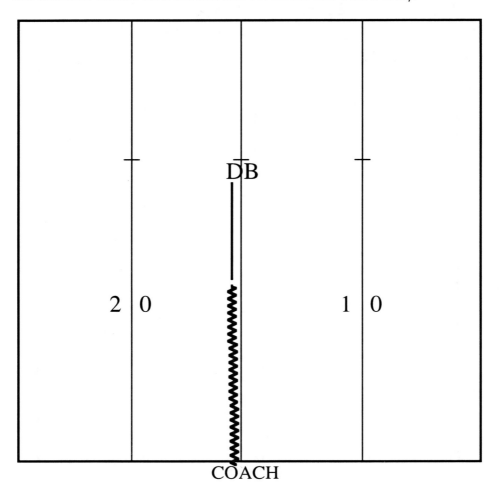

Drill #80: Deep Ball

Objective: To develop the defensive backs' ability to cover a deep route

Equipment Needed: Three balls

Description: Place one offensive player five yards from the sideline. Align the one defensive back close to the receiver, facing the other direction with his hand on the receiver's hip. On the start command, the receiver will run down the field. The coach should throw the ball when receiver is 20 yards downfield. The defender will turn and trail the receiver on his inside shoulder, trying to squeeze him to the sideline and concentrating on the receiver's head and eyes. The defender will look back for the ball over his inside shoulder, while feeling for the receiver with his outside hand.

Coaching Points:
- The defender should be in a good stance.
- The defender should not turn back for the ball too early.
- The defender should always keep inside leverage on the receiver.
- The defender should not overrun the receiver.

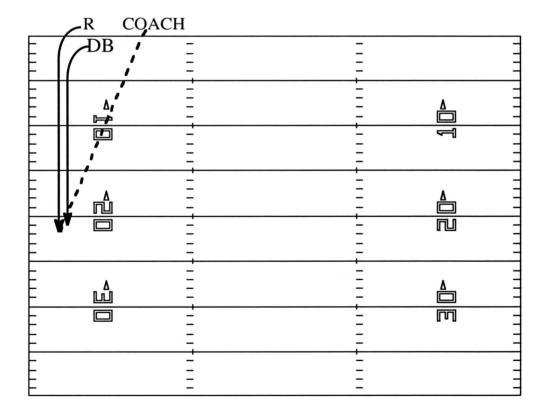

7

Group and Team Drills

Drill #81: Half Line

Objective: To develop the point-of-attack run defense

Equipment Needed: One ball

Description: Align eight players in their offensive positions (tight end, tackle, two guards, center, quarterback, fullback, and tailback), and align the six defensive players in their positions (strong safety, outside linebacker, end, nose, Mike, and Will). Have the offense run a play (e.g., power, iso, belly G, trap, or toss sweep). The defense should run a base front and stop the play, and then have the offense run the next play. Repeat the drill, or run the same play to the other side.

Coaching Points:
- The offense should run the play full speed.
- The defense should read and react to the play
- The coach could repeat the play to work on a missed assignment.
- The coach could run two huddles, one to the right and one to the left to increase the repetitions.
- The coach could take out the tight end to work on open end plays.

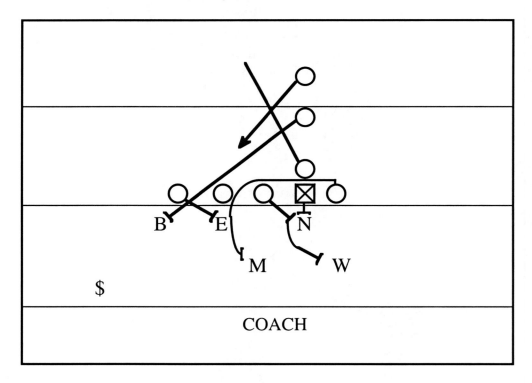

Drill #82: Inside Drill

Objective: To develop the defense's run defense

Equipment Needed: One ball

Description: Align nine players in their offensive positions (tight end, two tackle, two guards, center, quarterback, fullback, and tailback), and align the nine defensive players in their positions (two safeties, two outside linebackers, two ends, nose, Mike, and Will). Have the offense run a play (e.g., power, iso, belly G, trap, or counter). The defense should run a base front and coverage, then stop the play, and have the offense run the next play. Repeat the drill, or run the same play to the other side.

Coaching Points:
- The offense should run the play full speed.
- The defense should read and react to the play
- The coach could repeat the play to work on a missed assignment.
- The coach could run two offensive huddles to increase the repetitions.
- The coach could add a second tight end.

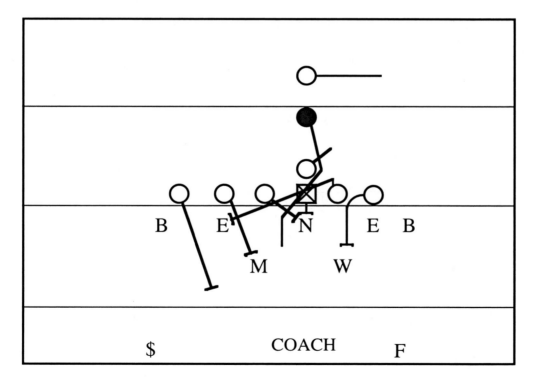

Drill #83: Outside Run Support

Objective: To develop the defense's run support responsibility versus outside run plays

Equipment Needed: One ball, five cones

Description: Align six players in their offensive positions (tight end, two wide receivers, quarterback, fullback, and tailback), and align the eight defensive players in their positions (two safeties, two outside linebackers, two corners, Mike, and Will). Have the offense run a play (e.g., toss sweep, inside veer, outside veer, speed option, reverse, and bootleg keep play). The defense should call a front and coverage, and then defend the play. After the offense runs the first play, they could run the next play or repeat the same play to the other side.

Coaching Points:
- The defense should call a front and coverage.
- The offense should run the play full speed.
- The defense should read and react to the play, but not tackle the back—break down and tag him on the hip.
- The coach could repeat the play to work on a missed assignment.
- The coach could run two offensive huddles to increase the repetitions.
- The coach could add a second tight end.
- The inside linebackers will not be blocked. (The inside linebackers have no contact; they read and react only.)

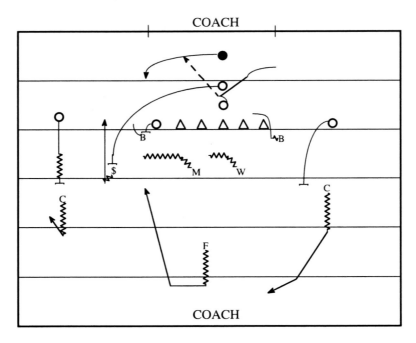

Drill #84: Pass Skel

Objective: To develop the defense's pass coverage responsibilities

Equipment Needed: One ball, five cones

Description: Align six players in their offensive positions (tight end, two wide receivers, quarterback, fullback, and tailback), and align the eight defensive players in their positions (two safeties, two outside linebackers, two corners, Mike, and Will). Have the offense run a play (e.g., dropback, sprint-out, play-action, or quick game passes). The defense should call a front and coverage, and then defend the play. After the offense runs the first play, they could run the next play or repeat the same play to the other side.

Coaching Points:
- The defense should call a front and coverage.
- The offense should run the play full speed.
- The defense should read and react to the play.
- The coach could repeat the play to work on a missed assignment.
- The coach could run two offensive huddles to increase the repetitions.
- The rush linebacker will not be blocked. (He should not hit the quarterback.)

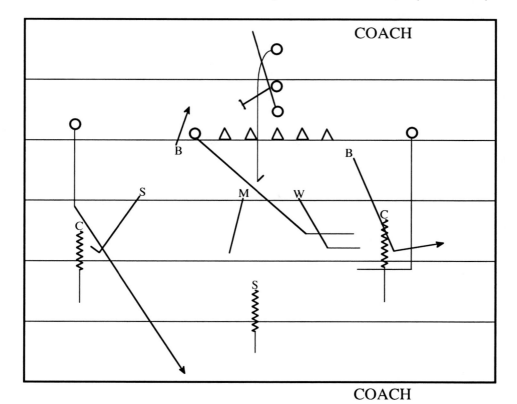

Drill #85: Front

Objective: To teach and review the defensive linemen's and linebacker's alignment and gap responsibilities

Equipment Needed: Five tires, one ball

Description: Align the five tires as the offensive line and one player as a tight end. Then align the seven defensive players in their positions (two outside linebackers, two ends, nose, Mike, and Will). The coach should call a front or stunt and coverage. The coach should give a "stance" command, and the plays should get into the proper stance and alignment. The coach should then move the ball, and the defensive player should move quickly through their assignments. Continue the drill by calling the next front, stunt, or blitz.

Coaching Points:
- The defensive player should be in a good stance.
- The coach could add a back to give the linebackers a read.
- The coach could repeat the play to work on a missed assignment.
- The coach could add a second tight end.

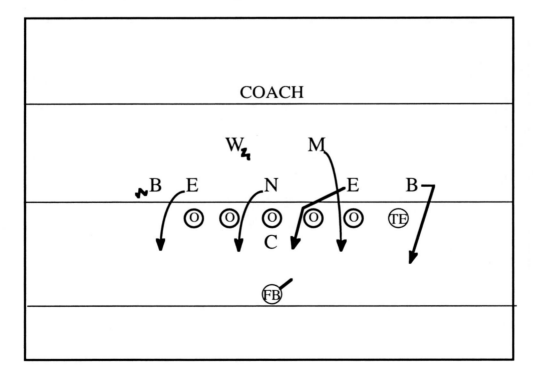

Drill #86: Dallas

Objective: To develop the linebacker's pass coverage responsibilities

Equipment Needed: One ball, five cones

Description: Align the five cones as the offensive line and four players in their offensive positions (tight end, slot receiver, quarterback, and one running back). Align the four linebackers in their positions. Have the offense run a play (e.g., dropback, sprint-out, play-action, or quick game passes). The defense should call a front and coverage, and then defend the play. After the offense runs the first play, they could run the next play or repeat the same play to the other side.

Coaching Points:
- The defense should call a front and coverage.
- The offense should run the play full speed.
- The defense should read and react to the play.
- The coach could repeat the play to work on a missed assignment.
- The rush linebacker will not be blocked. (He should not hit the quarterback.)

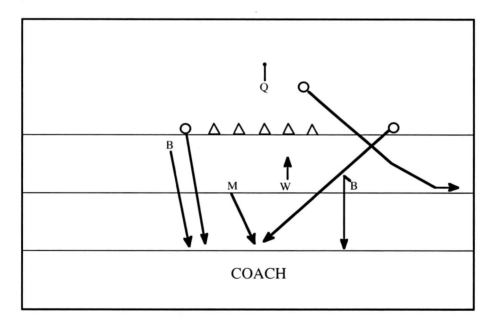

Drill #87: 3-on-3

Objective: To develop defensive players' ability to disengage off a block

Equipment Needed: Four cones, one ball

Description: Align the cones in a 10 x 10 yard square off the sideline. Align three blockers on the sideline with a running back three yards behind them. Align three defenders across from the blockers. On the go command, the offensive players should drive block the defenders, and the running back should run through the line of scrimmage. The defenders should attack the blocker and disengage off the blockers and tackle the ballcarrier.

Coaching Points:
- The players should be in a good stance.
- The running back should run between the cones.
- The defenders should try to knock the blockers back.
- The coach should match players up by size and ability.

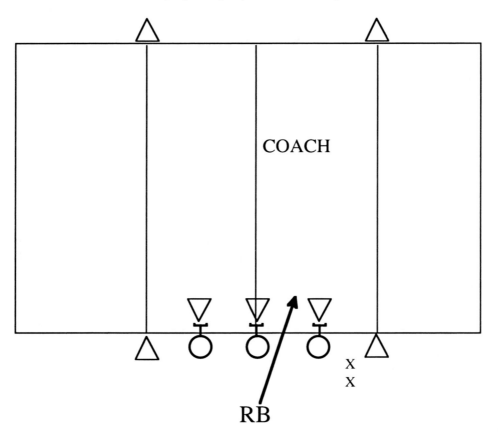

Drill #88: Spider

Objective: To develop defensive players' ability to disengage off a block

Equipment Needed: Four cones, one ball

Description: Align the cones in a 5 x 15 yard rectangle. Align an offensive lineman on the line of scrimmage with a running back three yards behind him a tight end five yards in front of him and a receiver five yard in front of him. Then, align three defenders across from the blockers. On the go command, the offensive players should drive block the defenders, and the running back should run through the line of scrimmage. The defenders should attack the blocker and disengage off the blockers and tackle the ballcarrier.

Coaching Points:
- The players should be in a good stance.
- The running back should run between the cones.
- The defenders should try to knock the blockers back.
- The coach should match players up by size and position.

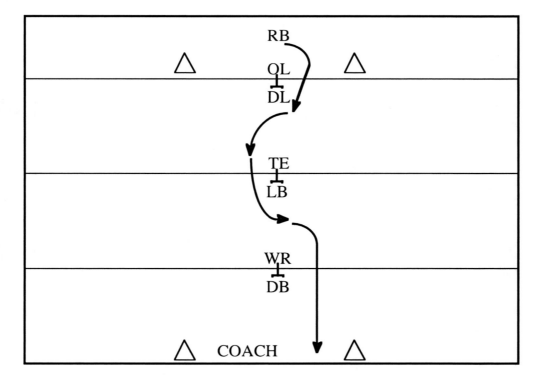

Drill #89: Last Hit

Objectives: To develop the will of the defensive players to get to the ballcarrier, and to teach proper angles of pursuit in the open field

Equipment Needed: Four cones

Description: Align two cones on the goal line, one on the front corner and one six yards from the sideline. Then, align the third cone at the 40-yard line on the sideline, and the fourth cone on the hash near the 30-yard line. Align the ballcarrier on the 40-yard line and the tackler on the hash. When the whistle blows, both players begin to run toward the corner of the end zone. The tackler must tag the ballcarrier before he crosses the goal line. Repeat the drill until all players get three repetitions.

Coaching Points:
- The coach can adjust the starting point for the tackler.
- The loser must do 10 push-ups.
- The ballcarrier can cut back.
- The players should switch line after each repetition.

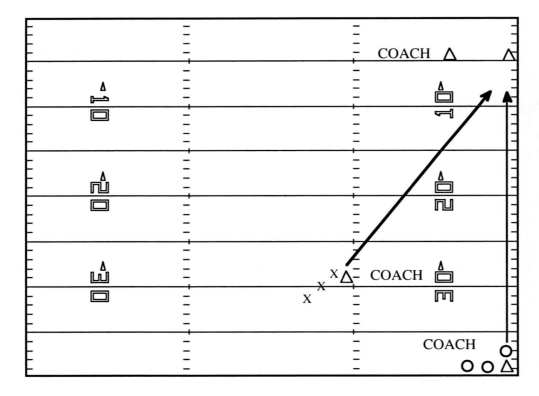

Drill #90: Full Speed Pursuit #1

Objectives: To develop the will of the defensive players to get to the ballcarrier, and to teach proper angles of pursuit in the open field

Equipment Needed: One ball

Description: One coach with a ball should align in a quarterback position at the 40-yard line in the middle of the field. The other two coaches should align on the sideline at the 40-yard line. The 11 defensive players should align in their positions across from the coach with the ball. On the go command, the quarterback should execute a down the line option track. The defensive players should take their read steps and then shuffle down the line. The quarterback should then throw the ball to the coach on the near sideline. The players should plant and run through their proper run support lanes. Repeat the drill until all players get three repetitions.

Coaching Points:
- The coach can run the play to either side.
- The players should run full speed through their proper run support lane.
- The players should break down at the end of the drill.

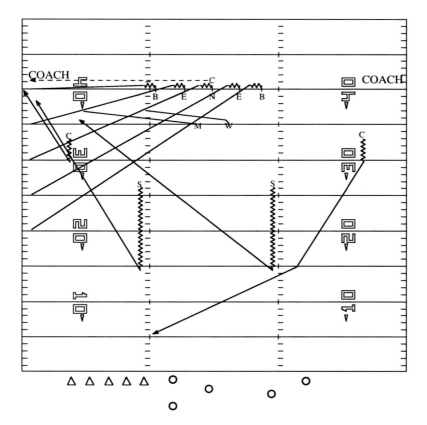

Drill #91: Full Speed Pursuit #2

Objectives: To develop the will of the defensive players to get to the ballcarrier, and to teach proper angles of pursuit in the open field

Equipment Needed: One ball

Description: One coach with a ball should align in a quarterback position at the 40-yard line in the middle of the field. The other two coaches should align on the sideline at the 40-yard line. The 11 defensive players should align in their positions across from the coach with the ball. On the go command, the quarterback should execute a dropback pass. The defensive players should take their read steps and then execute their dropback pass responsibility. The quarterback should then throw the ball to the coach on the near sideline. The players should plant and run through their proper run support lanes. Repeat the drill until all players get three repetitions.

Coaching Points:
- The coach can throw the ball to either side.
- The players should run full speed through their proper run support lane.
- The players should break down at the end of the drill.

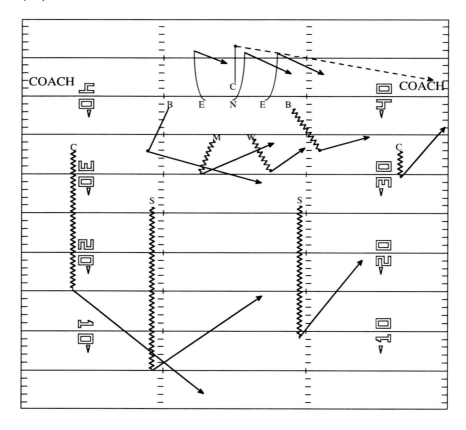

Drill #92: Full Speed Pursuit #3

Objectives: To develop the will of the defensive players to get to the ballcarrier, and to teach proper angles of pursuit in the open field

Equipment Needed: One ball

Description: One coach with a ball should align in a quarterback position at the 40-yard line in the middle of the field. The 11 defensive players should align in their positions across from the coach with the ball. On the go command, the quarterback should execute a dropback pass. The defensive players should take their read steps and then execute their dropback pass responsibility. The quarterback should then throw the ball downfield. The players should plant and run to the ball in the air. If the ball is picked off, the player yells "Oskie," and the entire defense turns and returns it into the end zone. If the ball hits the ground, the entire defense continues to the ball and breaks down. Repeat the drill with the next group.

Coaching Points:
- The coach can throw the ball to either side.
- The players should run full speed through their proper support lanes.
- The players should break down at the end of the drill.

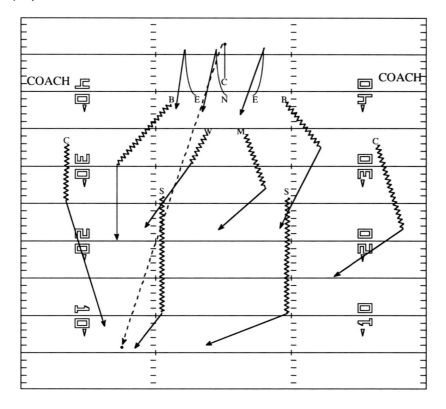

111

Drill #93: Agility Circuit

Objective: To develop the agility of the defensive players

Equipment Needed: Five half-moon bags, 10 cones

Description: This is a four-station rotation circuit training drill. Divide the players into four even groups, and then send the group to their starting station. For station one (agility bags), align the five bags perpendicular and three feet apart. At this station, the assigned drills are, high knees, lateral shuffle, and lateral run. At station two (four corners), place four cones in a square 10 yards apart. The assigned drill is: backpedal, carioca, sprint, carioca. For station three (ladder drill), align four cone in a line five yards apart. The assigned drill is suicide drill. At station four (mirror dodge), place two cones five yards apart. The assigned drill is mirror drill. Each station lasts for two minutes, and then they rotate.

Coaching Points:
- Station one: High knees run over the bags, lateral shuffle side step over the bags, and lateral run cross over the bags.
- Station two: Backpedal from cone one to cone two, carioca from cone two to cone three, sprit forward from cone three to cone four, and carioca from cone four back to cone one.
- Station three: For the suicide drill, the player should face the cone when you turn, and he should touch the line with his hand.
- Station four: The defensive player mirrors the offensive player by shuffling side to side; if the offensive player can fake out the defender, he should dodge him and pass the cone.

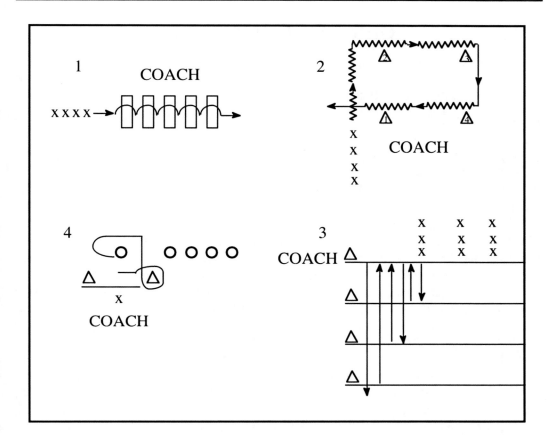

Drill #94: Tackle Circuit

Objective: To develop the defensive players' ability to tackle

Equipment Needed: 11 cones

Description: This is a four-station rotation tackling circuit drill. Divide the players into four even groups, and then send the group to their starting station. For station one (angle tackle), align two cone five yards apart. The players should form a line behind each cone. On the go command, the ballcarrier should run on a 45-degree angle to his left, the tackler should attack the ballcarrier and execute a proper angle tackle. Repeat the drill for two minutes. At station two (goal line tackle), place two cones on the goal line four yards apart and a third cone four yards away. The ballcarrier should align in front of the cone on the four-yard line. The tackler should align between the two cones on the goal line. On the go command, the ballcarrier will try to score between the two cones on the goal line. The tackler should attack the ballcarrier with a strong head-up tackle and drive the ballcarrier back. For station three (2-on-1 open field tackle), align two cones five yards apart and the third cone 10 yards away. On the go command, the ballcarrier should run forward. The tacklers should move forward in a low tackling position and keep the ballcarrier on their inside shoulders. When they get two yards from the ballcarrier, the tacklers should shimmy their feet and tackle the ballcarrier with the inside shoulder. At station four (shimmy tackle), place one cone on the sideline, one cone two yards from the sideline, and one cone on the numbers. The players should form two lines, one on the sideline and one on the numbers. On the go command, the tackler should run toward the second cone. When he gets to the cone, he should shimmy down, and the ballcarrier should move forward. The tackler should then chest-up tackle and club his arms up, executing a proper open field tackle. Each station lasts for two minutes, and then they rotate.

Coaching Points:
- Station one: For the angle tackle drill, the tackler should get his head across the body of the ballcarrier.
- Station two: For the goal line tackle, the tackler should keep his feet running on contact.
- Station three: For the 2-on-1 open field tackle, the tackles work proper angles of tackle.
- Station four: For the shimmy tackle, the tackler should use short, quick steps.

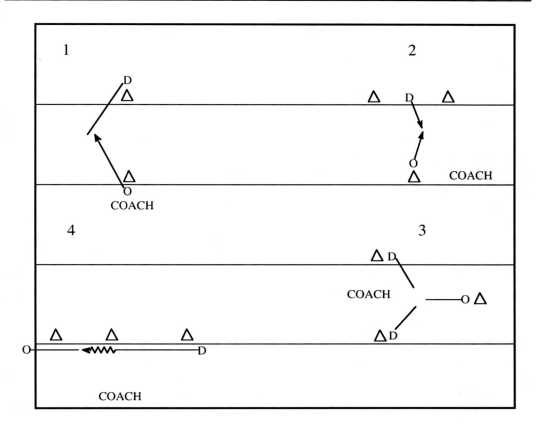

Drill #95: Turnover Circuit

Objective: To develop the defensive players' ability to force turnovers

Equipment Needed: 12 balls, cones

Description: This is a four-station rotation turnover circuit drill. Divide the players into four even groups, and then send the group to their starting station. For station one (punch drill), align two cones one yard apart. The players should form a line behind each cone. On the go command, the ballcarrier should run down the yard line, and the defender should chase the ballcarrier and execute a proper punch-up technique to knock the ball out. Repeat the drill for two minutes. At station two (strip drill), place two cones one yard apart. The players should form a line behind each cone. On the go command, the ballcarrier will run down the yard line, and the defender should chase the ballcarrier and execute a proper strip-down technique, pulling the ball loose. For station three (2-on-1 rip), align two cones five yards apart and the third cone five yards away. On the go command, the ballcarrier should run forward. The defenders should move forward in a low tackling position and keep the ballcarrier on their inside shoulders. When they get two yards from the ballcarrier, the tacklers should shimmy their feet and tackle the ballcarrier with the inside shoulder. The defender to the ballside should grab the ball and rip it out of the ballcarrier's hands. At station four (scoop and score), place one cone on the sideline. The players should form a line behind the cone. On the go command, the coach will roll a ball on the ground. The defender will attack the ball and scoop in up a turn and score past the cone. Each station lasts for two minutes, and then they rotate.

Coaching Points:
- Station one: For the punch drill, the defender should tackle with one arm and punch with the other.
- Station two: For the strip drill, the defender should secure the tackle and then strip the ball.
- Station three: For the 2-on-1 rip drill, both defenders should secure the tackle first.
- Station four: For the scoop and score drill, if the defender dose not scope the ball clean on the first try, he should fall on the ball and execute a proper fumble recovery.

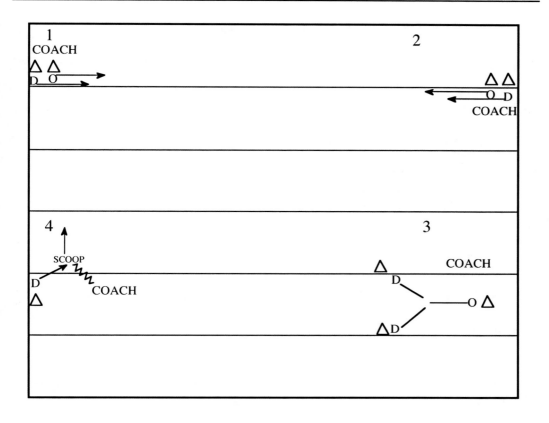

Drill #96: Screen

Objective: To develop the defense's ability to defend different screen, draw, and trick plays

Equipment Needed: One ball, an offensive team

Description: Align the 11 offensive players in their offensive positions, and align the 11 defensive players. Have the offense run a play (e.g., bubble screen, middle screen, tunnel screen, lead draw, or a trick play). The defense should call a front and coverage, and then defend the play. After the offense runs the first play, they could run the next play or repeat the same play to the other side.

Coaching Points:
- The defense should call a front and coverage.
- The offense should run the play full speed.
- The defense should read and react to the play, but they should not tackle the back—break down and tag him on the hip.
- The coach could repeat the play to work on a missed assignment.
- The coach could run two offensive huddles to increase the repetitions.

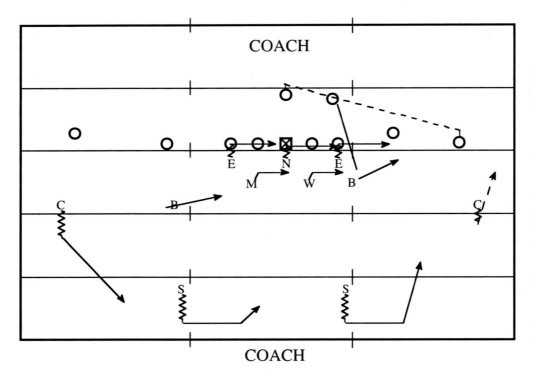

Drill #97: Team

Objective: To develop the defense's ability to defend different offensive plays

Equipment Needed: One ball, an offensive team

Description: Align the 11 offensive players in their offensive positions, and align the 11 defensive players. Have the offense run a play (e.g., inside runs, outside runs, dropback pass, and play-action pass plays). The defense should call a front and coverage, and then defend the play. After the offense runs the first play, they could run the next play or repeat the same play to the other side.

Coaching Points:
- The defense should call a front and coverage.
- The offense should run the play full speed.
- The defense should read and react to the play, but they should not tackle the back—break down and tag him on the hip.
- The coach could repeat the play to work on a missed assignment.
- The coach could run two offensive huddles to increase the repetitions.

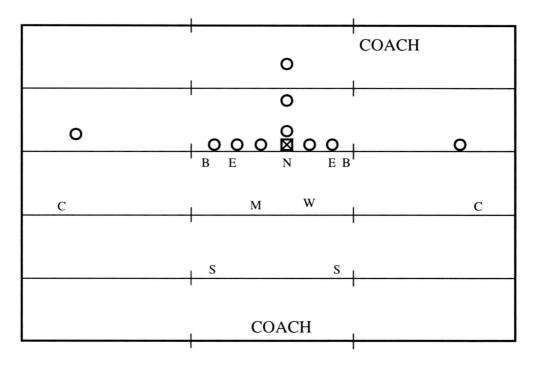

Drill #98: Goal Line

Objective: To develop the defense's ability to defend goal line plays

Equipment Needed: One ball, an offensive team

Description: Place the ball on the two-yard line. Align the 11 offensive players in their offensive positions, and align the 11 defensive players. Have the offense run a goal line play (e.g., inside runs, outside runs, or play-action pass plays). The defense should call a goal line front and coverage, and then defend the play. After the offense runs the first play, they could run the next play or repeat the same play to the other side.

Coaching Points:
- The defense should call a front and coverage.
- The offense should run the play full speed.
- The defense should read and react to the play, but they should not tackle the back—break down and tag him on the hip.
- The coach could repeat the play to work on a missed assignment.
- The coach could run two offensive huddles to increase the repetitions.

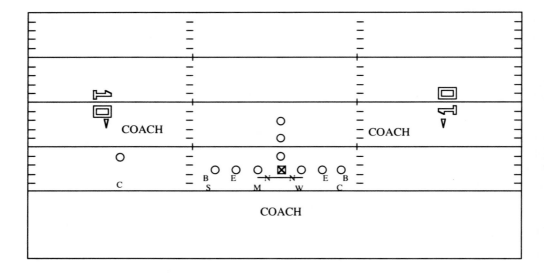

Drill #99: Two-Minute

Objective: To develop the defense's ability to defend against a hurry up two-minute offense

Equipment Needed: One ball, an offensive team

Description: Place the ball on the −20-yard line. Align the 11 offensive players in their offensive positions, and align the 11 defensive players. Have the offense run a hurry-up, no-huddle, two-minute drill. The defense should call a front and coverage, and then defend the play. After the offense runs the first play, they should run the next play or repeat the same play to the other side as quickly as they can.

Coaching Points:
- The defense should call a front and coverage.
- The offense should run the play full speed.
- The defense should read and react to the play, but they should not tackle the back—break down and tag him on the hip.
- The coach could repeat the play to work on a missed assignment.

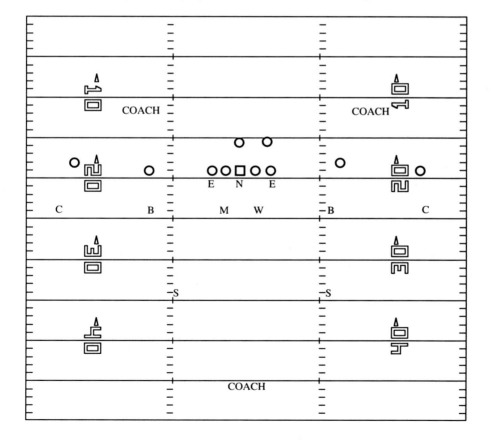

Drill #100: Overtime Challenge Drill

Objective: To develop the defense's ability to play great defense in overtime

Equipment Needed: One ball, an offensive team

Description: Place the ball on the 15-yard line, first-and-10. This drill should be run with your first defense versus your first offense. The offense should run their first play, and the drill continues until the offense scores or the defense stops them on downs or a turnover. (Follow your leagues rules for overtime play.)

Coaching Points:
- The defense should call a front and coverage.
- The offense should run the play full speed.
- The defense should read and react to the play.
- Play situation defense (first-and-10, second-and-8, etc.).
- Teach players to compete, and win the drill.

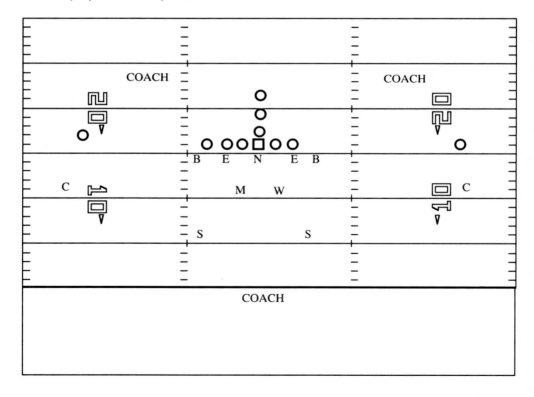

Drill #101: Green Bay's

Objective: To develop the defensive players' physical and mental toughness

Equipment Needed: Five cones

Description: Align a cone on each goal line, 20- and 40-yard line. Align the players on the goal line. On the first whistle, the players should do an up-down, and then run to the 20. When they get to the 20, they should chop their feet on the 20, and on the next whistle they repeat the up-down, and run to the 40. The drill continues down the field until they reach the opposite goal line.

Coaching Points:
- The players should chop their feet quickly.
- The players should perform a quick up-down.
- The players should sprint from cone to cone.

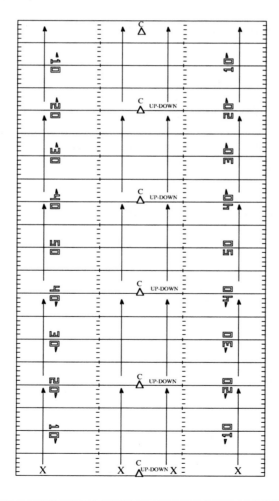

123

About the Author

James Pavao has been the defensive coordinator at Gainesville High School (5AAAAA) in Georgia since 2007. The Gainesville defense has been ranked as one of the top scoring defenses in the state of Georgia. In Pavao's six years as defensive coordinator, Gainesville has accumulated four regional championships, one state runner-up title, one final four appearance, and the 2012 state championship—resulting in a 67/13 record over the past six years.

Pavao started his coaching career in 1981 at Norwich University, where he was a graduate assistant offensive line coach. In 1982, he moved to Davidson College, where he coached defensive ends for two years, including two All-Conference players. In 1984, Pavao was hired to coach defensive ends at Princeton University, where two of his players received All-Ivy honors. Pavao then became the defensive coordinator at Maryville College, where he coached for 16 years and developed some of the top-ranked scoring defenses in Division III. In 2001, he left college coaching and was hired at Burke County High School in Georgia, where he coached for six years. During his tenure at Burke County, Pavao fielded four of the best scoring defenses in school history. From 2004 to 2006, his defenses had 10 shutouts. Pavao has used the 3-4 defense for over 25 years.

Born in 1959 in Providence, Rhode Island, Pavao graduated from East Providence High School, where he was an All-Conference football and baseball player. In 1981, he graduated from Norwich University, where he lettered for three years in both football and baseball.